ALAMO DEFENDERS

ALAMO DEFENDERS

A FRESH PERSPECTIVE ON THE HEROES OF 1836

JAMES W. BANCROFT

FRONTLINE
BOOKS

First published in Great Britain in 2024 by Frontline Books
An imprint of Pen & Sword Books Ltd Yorkshire – Philadelphia

Copyright © James W. Bancroft, 2024
ISBN 978 1 39900 991 1

Typeset by Lapiz Digital Printed and bound in the UK by
CPI Group (UK) Ltd, Croydon, CR0 4YY.

Printed on paper from a sustainable source by
CPI Group (UK) Ltd, Croydon, CR0 4YY

Pen & Sword Books Limited incorporates the imprints of Archaeology,
Atlas, Aviation, Battleground, Digital, Discovery, Family History,
Fiction, History, Local, Local History, Maritime, Military, Military Classics,
Politics, Select, Transport, True Crime, Air World, Claymore Press, Frontline
Publishing, Leo Cooper, Remember When, Seaforth Publishing,
The Praetorian Press, Wharncliffe Books, Wharncliffe Local History,
Wharncliffe Transport, Wharncliffe True Crime and White Owl.

For a complete list of Pen & Sword titles please contact

PEN & SWORD BOOKS LTD
47 Church Street, Barnsley, South Yorkshire, S70 2AS, England
E-mail: enquiries@pen-and-sword.co.uk
Website: www.pen-and-sword.co.uk

Or

PEN & SWORD BOOKS
1950 Lawrence Rd, Havertown, PA 19083, USA
E-mail: uspen-and-sword@casematepublishers.com

CONTENTS

Texas, they say, is a perfect paradise, and land is so uncommonly cheap that you can buy a farm for the price of a new bonnet; but earthquakes are very common, and the people are so very cruel, they kill each other with bowie knives in the streets, in open day, and so reckless that they keep singing 'Welcome to our gory bed', as if it was fine sport; so we have had to abandon all idea of it, as it would be mere madness to go there.

Letter Bag of the Great Western, or Life on a Steamer, 1840

Unhappy day, for ever to be deplored, that Sunday morning, March 6, 1836, when the undaunted garrison of the Alamo, victorious in so many assaults over twenty times their number, perished to the last man by the hands of those, part of whom they had released on parole two months before, leaving not one to tell how they first dealt out to multitudes that death which they themselves finally received.

Thomas Hart 'Old Bullion' Benton in a speech to the US Senate in 1836

In the history of almost every nation there are notable instances of heroism and self-sacrifice on the part of those who have risen in defence of their country in the hour of their greatest need. These men, generally drawn from all grades of life have no claim to be regarded as anything other than volunteers, pure and simple. They fought from no mercenary motive, nor even for the sake of renown; but from that stern sense of duty which alone can make men heroes in the truest meaning of the word.

Home Paper, 1897

INTRODUCTION

The siege and battle of the Alamo is something of a phenomenon, which has gripped the public imagination ever since it happened; and the site of the events in San Antonio has never lost its attraction for people of all walks of life and nationalities.

From 23 February to the morning of 6 March 1836 (a leap year), during the conflict known as the Texas Revolution, a garrison of frontiersmen of various backgrounds and from almost every region of the United States, and a number of Tejanos (Texas Mexicans), successfully defended a former mission complex on the other side of the San Antonio River from San Antonio de Bejar in Tejas (later Bexar and Texas), known as the Alamo, which they had utilised into a makeshift fort, against a large army of Mexican troops, who were on their way to give battle to the main force of American revolutionaries.

During the early hours of the last day of the siege Mexican forces stormed the fortress and killed all the men capable of bearing arms, including those who grew into American legends such as Colonels Davy Crockett, James Bowie and William Barret Travis. The very capable Mexican army was led by Generalissimo Santa Anna, who is described as one of the most emblematic figures in Mexican history, and had already become a legend in his homeland and beyond. Reports concerning his eventful career appeared frequently in British newspapers long before the Texas Revolution, and for many years afterwards.

What is not widely known is the fact that at least one in six of the defenders who helped the Texans were British-born, and of course most of the others had British ancestry. In fact, the family of garrison commander Colonel Travis descended from the county of Lancashire in north-west England. The Napoleonic Wars had cost the British treasury dearly, and in 1815, the year of the decisive battle of Waterloo, unemployment and poverty were rife in Great Britain. The Treaty of Ghent in that year ended the War of 1812 between Britain and the United States, and thus allowed the British to sail freely out to America.

1

These included Captain William Blazeby of Suffolk, who led the New Orleans Greys (Grays in American spelling) into the Alamo; and the unit included at least ten other Brits; and Major Robert Evans from Derry in Ireland, who, as master-of-ordnance in Captain William Carey's Artillery, was shot down in the chapel while trying to set light to the gunpowder during the final stages of the battle. However, this may have saved the lives of most of the women and children, who were hiding in adjoining rooms. Scotsman Sergeant John McGregor of the same unit is said to have played the bagpipes to accompany Davy Crockett on the fiddle to keep up the spirits and morale of their comrades during the siege. The artillery unit included at least eight other British-born men, and most of the Anglo-Americans in the New Orleans Greys and Carey's Artillery Company had previously taken part in the siege and battle of Bejar. Four Irishmen are believed to have travelled to San Antonio with Colonel James Bowie, and two Brits entered the Alamo with Colonel William Barret Travis. One of the seven members of the Mina Mounted Rangers (Bastrop) who fought and died at the Alamo was an Englishman, and a Scotsman arrived at the Alamo with Captain Philip Dimmitt's Company. At least two Anglo-Americans accompanied the Gonzales Ranging Company, the 'Glorious 32', which was the last unit to reinforce the garrison, and one of these was an Irishman who was also one of the 'Old Eighteen', who defended the Gonzales gun; the first engagement of the conflict.

In addition to this, it has not been possible to trace the place of origin of about twenty defenders, which suggests that they did not own land or have families in the United States; quite possibly because they were new immigrants. Several others are disputed.

Were the defenders of the Alamo heroes? Did any of them really want to give their lives for the cause of Texas independence? Or, as has been said by many historians, including Texans, were they only interested in protecting the land they had acquired or wanted to gain, retain the right to keep slaves, and would they have escaped if they had the chance to do so? These are questions that have been debated ever since the dust settled in San Antonio in 1836.

Whatever their motives were, it cannot be denied that, as volunteers not used to the wrath of war, they suffered the stress and anguish caused by the noise and danger of continuous cannon bombardments and sniper fire for nearly two weeks, suffering in arid conditions that sapped strength and the will to resist, and with very little sustenance. It was gruelling to the extreme. Each day they saw determined Mexican sappers digging trenches and tunnels all around the vulnerable fortress in their efforts to get at them; perhaps the first example of trench warfare in the history of conflict. Their nerves must have been stretched to breaking point as they wondered if their enemy might suddenly appear from out of the ground somewhere inside the compound they were defending.

As time passed they realised that no reinforcements were coming to help them and there was no chance to escape from an army with much more experience in warfare than they had, many of its officers being career soldiers, who were led by a very capable leader with a reputation of savage ruthlessness. In the early stages of the siege numerous couriers had come and gone from the garrison, so they knew it was possible to get away even if they did need an element of luck to succeed; but they stood their ground for as long as it was humanly possible to do so. Indeed the Mexican General de la Pena stated, 'Travis could have managed to escape during the first nights, when vigilance was much less, but this he refused to do.' Albert Martin left the Alamo on 23 February with Travis's 'To the people of Texas' letter, and as he had been wounded in the foot by an axe at Bexar, he could have used it as an excuse to get medical attention in Gonzales, but he returned to the Alamo as one of the 'Gonzales 32' on 1 March.

Sixty-two defenders are said to have tried to escape, but first-hand accounts suggest that this was towards the very end of the gruesome hand-to-hand fighting when all was lost and resistance was futile.

To suggest that men who endured such hardship for as long as they did were not gallant is extremely harsh. They looked out from battlements not ivory towers. To anyone who genuinely believes they were not brave men I repeat the words of a man who lost a whole family of his ancestors during the dreadful siege of Cawnpore (Kanpur) in India in 1857: 'I have come to realise that only those who have known paralysing fear, have felt the deepest abstract anxiety and been assured the perfect knowledge of complete and utter abandonment can fully understand what those poor souls went through.'

It is thought that Santa Anna had the bodies of the defenders burned to prevent them from gaining martyrdom status. However, he is known to have been shown the bodies of Travis, Crockett and Bowie, who were all reported to have been badly mutilated, and many of the defenders had been stripped and their bodies treated badly, so it is more likely that he decided that if they had been buried they could have been exhumed and the evidence exposed, so he decided to destroy them all. It has to be considered that the Mexican army were only at the start of the campaign, and it is known that Santa Anna desired a swift victory. He had already shown his frustration at how the siege had delayed his plans, so would he have been so concerned

3

about martyrdom and memorials? Surely if he did have such a train of thought he would also have taken the time to have his men destroy the chapel to prevent it from being a memorial – which, of course, it did eventually become.

Were the Mexicans who took part in the siege and battles of Bejar and the Alamo heroes? Some of the defenders who died on the Texan side were Mexicans known as Tejanos, and even James Bowie had been naturalised a Mexican. Alexander Edwin Sweet, a Canadian-born journalist who lived in San Antonio from 1849 to 1858, wrote: 'General Santa Anna and other high Mexican officers had a special spite at Bowie. He had married Maria Ursula Veramendi, the daughter of Governor Juan de Veramendi. The Mexicans thought because he had married into an aristocratic Mexican family he should have sided with them instead of with his own countrymen.'

Hundreds of Mexican soldadoes (soldiers), who must have been more concerned about providing for their families and concentrating on their own survival to take much interest in the political dysfunction that was causing so much trouble, gave their lives against men who were known to them as 'Pirates de la Tierra' – 'land pirates', invading the land that many of their fathers and grandfathers had fought and died for in the war for Mexico's independence from Spain during the difficult years leading up to and including 1821. It has to be said that during his speech to his men made after the Mexican Army had crossed the Rio Grande on 21 February 1836, Santa Anna's sentiments mirrored those that caused the British Task Force to be sent to repatriate the Falkland Islands in 1982. To add to that, Texans were continually thwarting Mexican laws, such as the keeping of slaves, which was prohibited in Mexico; although there were not many slaves in Mexico to begin with. The Mexican soldiers who marched towards San Antonio were proud to have been picked to join the forces of Santa Anna to liberate the part of their country where order needed to be restored and brought back under Mexican control.

Santa Anna undoubtedly had brutal instincts, but there are several examples of Mexican officers showing compassion towards the Americans. General Castrillon, though unsuccessful, pleaded for mercy on behalf of the captured defenders who had survived the initial fighting; General Almonte talked Santa Anna out of imprisoning Susanna Dickinson; one of the few survivors; and Colonel de la Pena stated: '… several women were found inside and were rescued by Colonels Morales and Minon'.

Santa Anna's hero was Napoleon Bonaparte; indeed he often referred to himself as 'The Napoleon of the West'. It seems that the

British defeat of the French during the Peninsular Wars caused him to harbour anti-British sentiments, for, although there had not been any battles between British and Mexican troops he 'has openly insulted the British flag by exhibiting it in his ballroom among trophies taken from the enemy. Whether he ever took it or not we do not know, but the British resident has protested against the insult.' It has to be said that without Santa Anna's stern leadership Spain may well have succeeded in forcing Mexico back under its influence.

During the Greco-Persian Wars, the battle of Thermopylae in Greece took place in the year 480 BC, when the Greek King Leonidas and his three hundred Spartans held out for three days against thousands of Persians under Xerxes I. The siege of the Alamo is rightly remembered as 'The Thermopylae of America'. Indeed, the defenders of the Alamo held out for much longer than the Spartans. It must also be compared to the numerous sieges suffered by the British during the reign of Queen Victoria, which began in the year after the Texas Revolution.

The Texas Revolution was not the first time the region had tried to break away from Mexico, and in the beginning of this work I have tried to concentrate on the history of Coahuila y Tejas and its wild uncertain times before the revolution broke out, to give the reader an idea of the kind of place the defenders fought for, and I have included background information concerning the participants, to try to bring everything into perspective.

For five decades I have collected information concerning courage and achievement that has now become the JWB Historical Archive; possibly one of the largest independent libraries of its kind. The documentation is almost entirely concerning the history of my own country, but one other event has found its way into it – the battle of the Alamo – mainly because of the number of Brits who took part. I have read and discussed everything I could about the subject, and I have tried as much as possible to tell the events in the first place by studying the original sources and primary literature. By doing so I was able to discover, among other things, that the first meeting between Captain Albert Martin and Colonel Juan Almonte was actually at a small bridge on what is now East Crockett Street, much closer to the Alamo and further north than the bridge on East Commerce Street where it was thought to have taken place and where it is commemorated at the junctions of East Commerce Street and Losoya Street.

Historians down the years have found some degree of discrepancy with every eyewitness account that has ever been written concerning the events at the Alamo. Moot points are blown out of all proportion, with no possibility of finding an answer, so in an attempt to avoid throwing even more mud in the water I have used the accounts of those who were present at a certain event whenever possible, and when more than one person witnessed or took part in an incident I have used the account of the person who I believe is most likely to have been in the best position to see, remember and record it; and is most relevant to the overall story.

I have always believed that a man who can be considered to have been a defender of the Alamo remains so until proven without doubt that he was not, and it must be confirmed where he was if he was not at the Alamo on 6 March 1836. I take the view that it is not appropriate to dismiss any of them without such proof; and I could be doing them an injustice if I did so. Absence of evidence is not evidence of absence.

A similar case can be made for several people associated with the battle of the Alamo, including Jesse Benton, who is not universally accepted as being a defender, and his name does not appear on the 'Spirit of Sacrifice' cenotaph in San Antonio. He is known to have been a friend of Davy Crockett, and he was with Crockett's unit when it left Nacogdoches to travel to the Alamo, from where he wrote a letter on the day before Santa Anna's army arrived there. It was suggested in the *Louisiana Advertiser* for 28 March 1836 that he was one of the men executed with Crockett after the battle. There is no proof that he left the Alamo at any time after the Mexican army arrived, so if he was not at the Alamo – where was he? And is omitting him an injustice?

By the same token it is my opinion that an account of the defence of the Alamo has to be considered to have been provided by a genuine eyewitness until proven without doubt that the teller of the story was an imposter or romancer. Therefore, I have used some accounts that are considered controversial, but which have never been proven without doubt not to be authentic.

I have expressed some personal views on certain incidents and aspects of the events; but in this work it is my intention to be informative to the general reader, and to give an unbiased point of view with a fresh British perspective.

In particular, it is my tribute to all the gallant and resourceful men and women who became caught up in one of the most poignant and tragic events in the history of the United States of America.

James W. Bancroft, 2024

COAHUILA Y TEJAS

The vast region north of the Rio Grande from Mexico now known as Texas was originally named Tejas after a tribe of native Indians, and the district that is now the City of San Antonio de Béxar became the centre for the work of Franciscan monks. It was officially founded on 5 May 1718, and Friar Antonio de Olivares (1630–1722) organised the establishment and construction of the San Antonio de Valero Mission. Apparently, at one time the facade at the front of the Alamo chapel displayed the year 1757, but other parts are thought to have been built earlier. Four of their missions have survived to this day. The Presidio (fort) was ordered to be built by Martin de Alarcon, who was twice the governor of Coahuila y Tejas from 1709 to 1719, and a detail of Spanish soldiers did all the work, mainly to provide protection against native Indian raids, particularly by the Comanches. The town expanded quickly. Juan Leal Goraz (1676–1742) became the first mayor in 1731, and the church of San Fernando was built in 1782. At the time of the Texas Revolution the town had an estimated seven thousand inhabitants.

The San Antonio de Valero Franciscan complex was situated on the eastern, or opposite side of the San Antonio River from the town, and there was a small village consisting of 'old fabric' buildings to the south-west. The complex served as home to missionaries and their Indian converts for nearly seventy years. In the early 1800s the Spanish military stationed a cavalry unit there and the soldiers referred to the old mission as the Alamo, or Álamo de Virginia, being Spanish for cottonwood, and was named after their home town of Alamo de Parras de la Fuente at Coahuila in Mexico. The first recorded hospital in Texas was established in the two-storey Long Barracks at the Alamo, parts of which still exist. The Alamo was home to both Revolutionaries and

Royalists during Mexico's struggle for independence and the Mexican military continued to occupy the Alamo until the Texas Revolution.

John Dunn Hunter (1796–1827) was a Cherokee leader around the time of the Fredonian Rebellion (21 December 1826 to 23 January 1827); which was the first attempt by Anglo settlers in Texas to break away from Mexico. The mostly undiscovered 'desolate waste of country' attracted many pioneers and adventurers like him. While in England he wrote an account that was published in London in 1824 under the title *Memoirs of a Captivity among the Indians of North America*.

The *Sydney Gazette* for 12 March 1828 published the following article concerning him, which gives a good account of Tejas at the time:

This extraordinary man, whose praiseworthy exertions to ameliorate the condition of the American Indians, obtained for him, while in this country, so many friends, has been very ably vindicated from the character of an imposter by the following article in an American paper.

I first saw Hunter in Nacogdoches, in the early part of last summer. His narrative, the reputation it had given him, and the charge which had so suddenly blighted his fresh fame, were all unknown to me, and little did I expect to meet him in the wilds of Texas. His countenance and demeanour, before I knew who he was, drew my attention; and though no physiognomist, nor pretending to any usual tact in penetrating the character through the external appearance, I was aware, and notwithstanding the plainness of his dress, and the simplicity of his manners, that I was in the society of a highly intelligent man, and a gentleman.

He was called Doctor Hunter. He had just returned from the city of Mexico, where he had been endeavouring to obtain a grant of land for numerous tribes of Indians, which had formed a kind of political alliance, at the head of which was Richard Fields, the principal Chief of the Cherokees. Fields himself had been to Mexico for that purpose, and had obtained a promise that the grant should be made. Hunter endeavoured to obtain the promise, but without success; the Mexicans having granted to impresarios the greater part of the promised-land.

He returned by land over a desolate waste of country that would have intimidated a less energetic and enterprising man. He brought back feelings of the strongest disgust towards the Government, and harassing fears lest the Indians, who were extremely irritated by the treachery practised upon them, and who were determined to have the land by force, if it could not be obtained otherwise, should declare open hostilities, and massacre the Americans who were settled upon it.

Such had been the injustice and tyranny of the local officers in Texas, sanctioned and supported as they were by the Government, that nothing but a consciousness of their own weakness had restrained the

Americans from open resistance. Now, therefore, was the moment to strike, at once to secure themselves from massacre on the part of the Indians, and throw off the despotic yoke which had galled them to the quick. An alliance was formed between a respectable portion of the Americans, for the benefit of all, and Hunter, with Fields, and several other chiefs, on behalf of the Indians.

The history of that short-lived struggle for independence is well known to most of our readers, and I will therefore only say that Hunter's conduct throughout was faithful, active, and energetic. On several occasions, when imminent danger was apprehended, he acted in a manner that convinced every person who saw him that his courage was equal to his enterprise. At the time when the few faithful adherents to the independent standard were surrounded on every side by their enemies, a runner was sent to the Cherokees to urge them to come instantly to the succour of their allies, at Nacogdoches. Fields and Hunter steadied every nerve to rouse the faithless Indians to the performance of their reiterated promises, and their solemn obligation by treaty, but in vain.

The emissaries of the Mexican government had been among them, and the renewed promise that the land they contended for would be granted, with other and great advantages, seduced them from their faith, and thus rendered the revolution abortive. Hunter finding every effort fruitless, for the few who had been brought over were unwilling to act with so small a force, left them, saying he would go alone, and share the fate of his American friends at Nacogdoches.

His opposition to the treachery excited their deadly hostility. They proceeded to join the Americans, accompanied by two Indians. He stopped at a creek near the Anadagua village, to let his horse drink, and while thus unguarded in his security, one of his savage companions shot him with a rifle in the shoulder. His horse started, and he fell into the Creek. The monster raised another fatal weapon, and while the unfortunate Hunter implored him not to fire, for it was hard, he said, to die by the hands of his friends, sent his extraordinary spirit to appear before an unerring tribunal.

Hunter was a person about the middle size, stoutly made, and apparently of much strength. His countenance, though far from handsome, was very expressive. The strong lines of a marked character were his, indicating the powerful feelings and the glowing enthusiasm that belonged to the man. His manners were in general quiet, grave, and gentlemanly, but they would burst out into singular vivacity when his feelings were roused; and then at times his high excitement would render him master-less of himself, and while it made him eloquent, in gesticulation, deprived him of all command over his words. Any discussion relative to the situation and character of the Indians would rouse the level calm of his ordinary manner into a storm that agitated his entire soul. Grave, deliberate, and intelligent on every other subject, the moment that chord was touched his enthusiasm and ardour overpowered the sluggishness of calculating investigation, and his imagination burned with the distant prospect of the civilization and happiness of the persecuted Indians – the long-cherished object of his philanthropic ambition.

There was no regular army to protect the people who had settled in Tejas against attacks by Comanche Indians and other tribes, or bandit gangs. Comanches were expert horsemen, and dreadfully warlike, and even their name is derived from a native Indian word meaning 'anyone who wants to fight me all the time'.

In 1823, Stephen Fuller Austin (1793–1836), an impresario who became known as the 'Father of Texas', after whom the modern city is named, organised small groups of horsemen whose duties required them to range over the countryside, and who thus became known as 'Rangers'. In early August 1823, Austin wrote that he would '... employ ten men ... to act as rangers for the common defence ... the wages I will give said ten men is fifteen dollars a month payable in property ...'

Austin returned to Tejas on 13 July 1835, after having been imprisoned in Mexico City, and helped organise a council to govern the unit. On 17 October, at a consultation of the Provisional Government of Texas, a resolution was proposed to establish three companies of Texas Rangers, totalling sixty men, and within two years the Rangers grew to more than three hundred. The unit protected the Texas frontier against Indian attacks on the settlers, and during the Texas Revolution they served mainly as scouts, spies, couriers and guides, and undertook general support duties. In 1866, an English Texas Ranger named Captain Flack, who had roamed all over Texas for fifteen years, gave a good idea of what life was like in the region when he wrote:

When Texas was a Mexican province it was scarcely inhabited at all by civilized people. A stray fort here and there, as at Anahuac and Velasco, was garrisoned by Mexican soldiers; and near them under the protection of their guns, a few adobe (wattle and daub) houses were built. Two towns, San Antonio de Bexar and San Felipe de Bexar, with the missions of Refugio and San Patricio established by some Jesuit priest as early as 1660 were the principal inland settlements.

The rest of Texas was roamed by Indian tribes, who followed the buffalo herds and wild horses, which at that time fed down to the sand hills on the shores of the Mexican Gulf. In the winter, when their mountain homes on the San Saba range were visited with frost and snow, the savage tribe of Comanche Indians were accustomed to move their lodges and families down towards the sea coast, where the weather was always like summer, except now and then for a day or two when the north winds prevailed. Two other powerful and warlike tribes, the Lipans and Apaches, also had their winter hunting-grounds towards the Texan coast. All these Indians claimed Texas for their hunting ground, and despised the Mexicans, killing them whenever they met them, and appropriating their horses, cattle and property generally, whenever they came across them.

The first blame for this violence rests with the early European settlers. In self defence alone is force justifiable, even towards savages. About the year 1820, Stephen F. Austin, an American citizen, obtained a large grant of land from the Mexican Government, on condition that he settled upon it, in a given time, three hundred families from the United States of America. The Mexicans knowing well that the country was useless to them so long as the Indians wandered over it as they pleased, killing their people and destroying their property; and they hoped that the rifles of the Americans would hold in check the savages, so that in time, their own people might settle in the country in safety.

However, their plans backfired with dreadful consequences!

***

In his *The Rise, Progress and Prospects of the Republic of Texas* (2 volumes), of 1841, William Kennedy wrote of how precarious life was in Texas during the years leading up to the Revolution, and the hardships endured by Moses and Stephen Austin:

Under Spanish misrule, Texas lay a boundless waste. A few missions and presidios, or small forts garrisoned by convicts served merely to maintain the claim of dominion over it. The Anglo-Americans, however, broke a commercial road through it from their western settlements to Central Mexico. But the fears with which that bold and adventurous people inspired their Spanish neighbours, are plainly expressed in a declaration of a Mexican ruler that 'He would forbid the birds flying across the frontier.' Yet the Anglo-Americans continually pressed on the Mexican territory till at last they were allowed to establish themselves within it. The schemes and attempts of Aaron Burr and Philip Nolan to revolutionise Mexico, and make the most of the frontier territory, fully show how deeply rooted were the causes which have led to the independence of Texas. The European world is hardly aware how long the seeds of revolution lay germinating in that soil. A plot was also entered into in 1826 by the Cherokees to seize a part of Texas, but was frustrated by treachery and vigilance of the white men. The leader of the Cherokees on that occasion was Hunter, whose account of his early captivity among the Indians made him the lion of London coteries a few years back.

The truth of his narrative was, at the time of its publication, positively denied in the United States, yet Hunter's last efforts bear witness at least to the sincerity of his attachment to the red men. He was murdered at the instigation of Bowles, a half-bred Indian, and chief of the Cherokees, who deserted the cause of the insurgents.

We know not the date of a liberal grant of 21,000 square leagues of land in Texas, said to have been made by the Mexican government to one Edmund Keene. The first grant of the kind that led to practical consequences was that made in 1821 to Moses Austin, a New-Englander of the go-ahead school, and an experienced backwoodsman. Being unfortunate as a merchant and miner in the United States, he obtained, in 1799, a conditional grant of land, with a lead mine in Upper Louisiana, or, as it is how called, Missouri.

After winding up his affairs Moses Austin removed his family, with a number of others, from Wythe County, by a new and almost untried route, down the Kenhawa River, in 1799, and originated the settlement of the present county of Washington in Missouri. To comprehend the difficulties attendant on this undertaking, it is necessary to bear in mind that to Missouri improvement was at that period, a stranger. From Louisville to St Genevieve between which points were embraced the present States of Indiana and Illinois, the whole tract was a wilderness, traversed by prowling savages only with the exception of a few French settlers on the Wabash and Kaskaskia. The family of his nephew, Elias Bates, was the first, and his own the second, that ever spent a winter at Mine-a-Burton. Durham Hall, the seat that Mr Austin raised in the uncultivated wilds, was for years the centre of the domestic virtues and expanded benevolence. His upright character and public spirit won for its owner the affectionate respect of the early settlers. Industry was considerately stimulated and generously rewarded under his influence and the beautiful village of Herculaneum springing up as if by magic, indicated the prosperity which had repaid the meritorious exertions of him who might be termed the genius of the place. Unhappily, the exercise of those qualities which were most honourable to his nature was followed by a second ebb of his fortunes; yet, though declining in the vale of years, his native ardour and buoyancy of spirit were neither chilled nor depressed. In the hour of adversity he turned his eyes towards Texas, and organised a plan for drawing forth the neglected treasures of its exuberant soil by the introduction of Anglo-American labour.

The idea of expanded benevolence in the backwoods savours perhaps a little of conceit. Spacious as those regions may be, they afford little room to the social virtues. It cost Austin much time and trouble to overcome the suspicious and dilatory habits of the Spanish officials. He succeeded at last, however, in obtaining permission to settle three hundred families in Texas and immediately set out on his return to Missouri. The journey homewards was attended by extreme suffering and hardship. From Bexar to the Sabine, Texas was then a total

12

solitude, the settlements at Nacogdoches and its vicinity having been destroyed by the Spaniards in 1819. Robbed and deserted by his fellow travellers, Austin was left alone on the prairies, nearly 200 miles from any habitation, destitute of provisions and the means of procuring them. In this wretched situation, with nothing to subsist upon but acorns and pecan nuts, he journeyed onwards for eight days, constantly exposed to the weather, at the most inclement season, swimming and rafting rivers and 'creeks', until he reached the hospitable roof of an American settler, 20 miles from the Sabine. Worn down with hunger and fatigue, he was unable to proceed further. His constitution had received a shock, from which it never recovered.

After recovering his strength, he resumed his journey, and arriving in Missouri in spring, commenced preparations for removal to Texas, but a cold which had settled on his lungs, produced an inflammation that tormented his existence, a few days after the gratifying intelligence was communicated to him of the approval of his petition by the Spanish authorities at Monterey. He died on the 10th of June, 1821, in his fifty-seventh year, leaving as a last injunction to his son Stephen, to prosecute his plan of Texan colonisation.

Stephen Austin, on who devolved the task of establishing the intended colony, had now difficulties to encounter in the disturbed state of the government. Above two years elapsed before he could obtain the confirmation of the grants made to his father, or go through the official forms necessary to perfect his title to the land. At length, in 1824, the stipulated number of three hundred families was located in the best part of Texas, between the rivers Brazos and Colorado. Let it not be imagined, however, that these settlers sat down at once in affluence and comfort; they had to endure the hardships inevitably awaiting those who march in the vanguard of colonisation, and, though adapted by previous habits to such trials – though occupying a fruitful soil, a mild climate, and on a navigable river, yet many of them lost all patience and returned to Louisiana.

Hitherto, the duties which devolved upon Stephen Austin, though calculated to exhaust the patience and depress the spirit, were merely preparatory to the great work of colonisation which had been grievously interrupted and embarrassed. An unlucky fatality seemed from the beginning to weigh upon the enterprise. The commanders of the first vessels that sailed with stores from the United States, owing probably to the inaccuracy of the charts, were unable to make the place of rendezvous at the mouth of the Colorado. One cargo which was safely landed was destroyed by the Comanche Indians, in the autumn of 1822, and four men massacred. The settlers were compelled to bring seed corn from the Sabine, a distance of several hundred miles, or to purchase it at Bexar, where it was scarce and dear. They were destitute of bread; and sugar and coffee were only present to them in hope.

Their dependence was on the game of the country – buffalo, bear, deer, wild turkey and mustangs. But buffalo hunting was perilous among unchastised tribes of Indians, a failure in the mast of the woods had rendered the bears meagre and scarce, and the venison likewise was in bad condition. Wild horses, however, were fat and very abundant, and it is estimated that 100 of them were eaten during the first two years. In this condition of affairs, the withdrawal of a portion of the colonists will occasion little surprise.

Stephen Austin subsequently obtained other grants and although tormented by the government, and at one time imprisoned for a year in Mexico, he nevertheless persevered, until he had settled nearly 1,200 families in Texas. He must be regarded as the founder of that Anglo-American state, the existence of which began but eighteen years ago. Many tried to follow his example, and obtained grants for that purpose from the Mexican government; but few of them proved successful. Experiments were made with colonies of Swiss, Germans, and of Irish. The Irish colonies, which had never a healthy appearance, were dispersed in the war with the Mexicans. The Anglo-Americans alone withstood the storms which assailed the young settlements, and have firmly taken root in the soil.

The Mexican and Anglo-American differ so widely in sentiment and habits that it would be hardly possible for them to move in concord as members of the same community. Mistrust and complaints soon arose between them. But it must be confessed that the petty tyrants who first drove the settlers to appeal to arms were themselves Anglo-Americans in the Mexican service. These first differences were easily adjusted; but the proof which the colonists gave of high spirit and conscious freedom was not lost on the Mexican Government; and stealthy means were resorted to for the purpose of increasing the military force in Texas, aimed at fixing the fetters on the Anglo-Americans, without provoking an open rupture with them. But the colonists felt the dissembled hostility of their rulers, and armed themselves at once to save their liberties.

Coahuila de Tejas became the most northern of the constituent states. Tejas continued to be colonised by American and Anglo settlers and by the early 1830s the Anglo-American population had increased to 30,000. Eventually, the Mexican government saw the influx of so many foreign nationals as a threat and when Santa Anna abolished the original constitution it removed most of the Texan rights and they became disillusioned and rebellious.

2

EL EJERCITO MEXICANO

Santa Anna held high office in Mexico from 1837 to 1855, and was the nation's president on several occasions. He called himself 'the Napoleon of the West', and his time in power is remembered as 'the Age of Santa Anna'. He could be a determined ally and a ruthless enemy – to the same cause at different times for both the Liberals and Conservatives; and he took no consideration of the fact that it was on the Sabbath Day he chose to take the lives of the Alamo defenders. However, without his presence and influence Spain may well have succeeded in reconquering Mexico and bringing it back under its rule.

An obituary appeared in the *Alta California* of 10 July 1876, and in various newspapers around Britain and the Empire, concerning the life of Antonio de Padua María Severino López de Santa Anna y Pérez de Lebrón, the first part of which read:

> Lopez de Santa Anna was born on 21 February 1798 [1794], at Xalapa [the capital city in the Mexican State of Vera Cruz; which he called 'Heroic' Vera Cruz].
>
> He first appeared in public life during the Mexican war for independence, in 1821. In 1822 he expelled the Spanish from the state of Vera Cruz, of which state he was appointed Governor. During the same year Iturbide, having proclaimed himself Emperor, attempted to depose Santa Anna, who resisted the domination of the mock emperor and adhered to the Republic, and he was subsequently instrumental in procuring the downfall of the Empire.
>
> He was, however, defeated soon after by the Federals, and remained in retirement on his estate at Xalapa until 1828, when he headed the revolt against the lawful President Pedrada, in the interest of Guerrero, who gave him command of the troops sent against the Spanish invaders under Barradas, whom he captured in Tampico, in September 1820.

Santa Anna then united with Bustamente, and overthrew Guerrero in 1832, then in 1833 overthrew Bustamente, and declared for his old opponent, Pedrada, whom he had himself deposed.

In the same year as he was elected president he put down an insurrection, and, abandoning the Federalists, took part with his old enemies, the Centralists, with the evident intention of ultimately making himself Emperor. In 1835 he overthrew the Republican army near Zacatecas [fought on 11 May 1835], destroyed the State organisation, and abolished the Constitution.

He was an inspiring speaker, although Colonel de la Peña was of the opinion that he 'loses battles and wins the wars with words'. The *Sydney Monitor* for 24 February 1830, stated: 'The Expedition of Ferdinand [VII] of old Spain against his rebellious South American Colonies, has at length landed at Vera Cruz. The following is the Proclamation of Santa Anna, the general of what the invading army calls 'the insurgent enemy':

Soldiers! – The Spanish expedition, so often announced as preparing at Havannah [Havana in Cuba] for the invasion of our territory, has at length arrived; and these vile slaves of the greatest of despots have already dared to set their feet upon our soil at Cape Roquel. Obstinate in her purpose to re-conquer this country, Spain has not ceased to provide the means for eventually accomplishing it; and this army which now presents itself, is the vanguard of the great expedition which she has prepared as the result of her arduous labour. But it is the last attempt which will be made by that imbecile nation to deprive us of independence.

Soldiers! These perfidious men provoke us to an encounter. They will find to their sorrow that you do not shrink from them, but that you are already on the march to accept the challenge! They threaten you with death; but the sharp edge of your swords will infallibly cause them to perish by hundreds, and to bite the soil which they have dared to profane; insomuch that not an individual will remain to witness the destruction which their rash enterprise has merited!

My Friends! A delightful field of glory opens before us, in which we will gather new laurels – valour and constancy, discipline, subordination, and order. Such qualities as these cannot deceive us. Always remember, that you fight for independence and liberty; and let those dear names urge you to combat with double ardour, till the triumph is achieved. That it will be achieved, who can doubt?

Soldiers! – It is better to die – to die a thousand deaths, if possible – than to suffer the hard yoke of oppression, which these tyrants seek to

impose. Independence or death! Let it glitter on your standards; let it be
the only sound which echoes through your camp, as it is and will be the
motto of your General.
   Antonio Lopez De Santa Anna
   Heroic Vera Cruz, 3 August 1829

The Mexican infantry consisted of two types of battalions. The
Permanente, as the name suggests, were permanent or regular
battalions; ten in total. After 1833 they were named after heroes of the
Mexican War of Independence. The *Activo* were active or National
Guard militia battalions, usually named from the geographical area
where they recruited. There were sixteen in total. The army was based
on a conscript system. Volunteers could enlist for eight years, while
draftees served for ten. The height of Mexican recruits was usually
5'4" - 5'8" (162–173cm). Perhaps the most professional element of the
Mexican Army was the *zapadores* or engineers.

The Mexican soldier served lengthy enlistment terms under harsh
conditions for low pay. Deserters generally received additional service
time for the first offence, and the second absence added service in
coastal garrisons; which was harsh punishment as they were usually
sent to unhealthy stations. In wartime, apprehended deserters faced
execution. Pay for line *soldados* was 15 pesos a month, from which
clothing and food allowances were drawn. *Cazadores* in the rifle
companies and the *granaderos* received one *peso* more.

The force that was to go to Tejas included veterans of numerous
campaigns, including the battle of Zacatecas in Mexico, fought on
11 May 1835, under Santa Anna, when the Centralist Mexican army
put down a Federalist rebellion under Francisco Garcia Salinas
(1786–1841).

The *soldado* wore a wool tail coat, cut at the waist, with wool pants.
The colours and style of the facings on sleeves and collars depended on
regiments and branch of service. The standard Mexican headgear was
a shako. During the 1830s, it was bell crowned. Shakos were designed
not merely for a military appearance, but as protection against sword
blows and the elements. Some units received a canvas summer or canvas
tropical white uniform, and, in many cases, they wore combinations of
this uniform and the wools. While brogans or shoes were issued, many
soldiers preferred sandals or to go barefoot on the march.

The standard infantry weapon of the Mexican army in 1836 was the
old East India pattern (Brown Bess musket) in .75 calibre, which were
purchased from Great Britain in large numbers. The muskets had no

sights, and the Mexican infantry had no marksmanship training. They used low-grade black powder which produced blinding smoke. Its only effective use was mass volley fire in the enemy's direction until they could come to hand-to-hand fighting with the bayonet.

Contemporary accounts from the Texas Campaign noted Mexican cartridges were often overcharged to give the weapon more punch. The result was an intimidating flash in the weapon's pan, stinging cheeks and eyes, and it had fierce recoil. Texan accounts claimed Mexican troops often fired from the hip to reduce the discomfort of the discharging weapon. As occurred in most armies, Mexican ordnance officers occasionally issued the wrong ammunition.

Mexico's cavalry units were 'light' (small men on small horses); similar to the Light Brigade in the British cavalry. During the nine years of hostilities between Texas and Mexico, the Texans developed a system of mounted tactics to deal with Mexican cavalry. Arms for the cavalry consisted of a wide variety of *escopetas* (short-barrelled carbines), swords, *espada anchas* (short swords), lariats and the lance. The lance was the deadliest and most reliable weapon a mounted soldier could carry. In several engagements, lancers almost proved fatal to the Americans, armed with swords and single-shot pistols.

Mexican officers normally deployed their artillery as a complete corps. No individual or battalion designations were used. The Mexican Artillery Corps contained some of the better-educated and trained *soldados*, but was hampered by poor equipment. The guns were heavy, and not easily transported. When in defensive positions, Mexican cannon could be quite effective, but on the offensive they became more of a hindrance than a help.

The care of the sick and wounded *soldados* was a concern of the government following the disastrous 1836 Texas War, when hundreds suffered needlessly from lack of a proper medical corps. Santa Anna retained the services of a North American doctor on the march from Saltillo, but the doctor later died.

The battle of the Alamo turned San Antonio into a garrison field hospital, and the commandant, General Juan Andrade, urgently requested 'medical supplies, bandages, thread and medical herbs' as well as an 'efficient doctor'. Andrade was forced to look elsewhere for medical assistance, bringing three American surgeons spared from the Goliad Massacre to assist. Upon arriving in Bexar one of them observed the '[Mexican] surgical department is shockingly conducted, not an amputation performed before we arrived … there has been scarcely a ball cut out as yet, almost every patient carrying the lead he received'.

Aside from wounds received on the battlefield, the *soldado* faced the usual variety of illnesses associated with the nineteenth-century military brought on by bad hygiene, fouled water and spoiled rations. Spotted itch, dysentery and yellow fever constantly reduced ranks. Rations in the 1836 Texas War consisted of hardtack, corn cakes, beans and flour, and a supplement of meat, which Italian-born General Vincente Filisola (1785–1850) noted was 'of poor quality, dry and not very nutritious and even harmful'.

The Mexican army quickly learned to live off the land, but even this was hampered by ongoing late payment for field troops. General Ramirez y Sesma, commanding the vanguard division of the 1836 *Ejercito de Operaciones*, was so pressed for fresh supplies and currency that he confiscated food stuffs from the villas and haciendas on his route to Bexar, and the division following found inhabitants resenting them because of Sesma's treatment of them.

In addition to the ration situation, the elements often conspired to increase the misery of the *soldado*. Where the government failed, individual initiative took over. The *soldadera* or female camp followers helped to supplement rations. A *chusmas* or mob of such women, often with children, marched with the Mexican military, much to the displeasure of several ranking officers, including General Filisola. These women provided 'home services', which included more than just physical activities. They secured clothing and extra rations, mended and cleaned equipment, and prepared meals. While many *soldaderas* were wives, others were less legitimate. Officers also brought *soldaderas* along. They were a tough, resourceful lot, and often paid for their unofficial status with their lives.

Critics often suggest that the *soldado* did not have the stomach to fight, and exposure to prolonged combat produced instant morale problems and desertion. One foreign observer noted that Mexicans could not manage a bayonet assault. The American historian Rodolfo Acuna characterised the Mexican *soldado* as 'ill-prepared, ill-equipped and ill-fed'.

Deserting was punishable by death, as was quoted in the general orders of the Second Brigade during its march towards Tejas on 1 and 2 January 1836, and is another example of how Santa Anna led by example: 'A deserter from the Toluca Battalion has been apprehended and remains safely in prison, so that he may be executed in the Brigade to which he belongs, thus complying with an order of his Excellency, the president, which provides that any individual caught committing a similar crime should be given the death penalty. All of which is transmitted through this order, so that it be read and understood by all members of this brigade, so that they may not plead ignorant of the law.'

However, Mexican soldiers are known to have demonstrated commendable courage and remarkable ruggedness, and bravery was a common trait among them. For instance, Sub-Lieutenant José Maria Torres of the *Zapadores* was mortally wounded while raising the Jimenez colours over the Alamo. Jose Maria Tornel (1795–1853), the Mexican secretary of War and Marine, was a well-educated man of letters, who was a patriotic Mexican and extremely anti-Anglo-American, stated: 'The superiority of the Mexican soldier over the mountaineers of Kentucky and the hunters of Missouri is well-known. Veterans of twenty years of wars cannot be intimidated by the presence of an army ignorant of the art of war, incapable of discipline and renowned for insubordination.' Mexico rewarded its troops with medals and badges for military service. These included the Star for the Defense of Texas (1836).

Among other senior officers of the Mexican Army who were present at the siege and assault on the Alamo were:

Colonel Juan Nepomuceno Almonte Ramirez was born on 15 May 1803 at Nocupétaro, in the Tierra Caliente region of Michoacán, Mexico, the illegitimate son of Mexican revolutionary hero, the Catholic priest Juan Morelos. His mother was an Indian woman named Brigida. He was educated in New Orleans, where he learned to speak English; and he was a lifelong supporter of Santa Anna. In 1824 he travelled to London as part of the Mexican delegation, and played a part in the arrangement and signing of Mexico's first business and amity agreement with England. When the Mexican government feared a revolt, he was sent to Tejas, and in the summer of 1834, having based himself in Nacogdoches, he compiled a detailed evaluation of all the departments of Tejas.

Colonel Jose Mariano Salas (1797–1867) was born in Mexico City. He joined the Royal Spanish Army while still a teenager in 1813 as a cadet in the Pueblo Infantry Regiment, and he saw his first action with the royalists putting down anti-Spanish rebels. He later fought with Santa Anna at the capture of Jalapa in Vera Cruz, the home town of Santa Anna and Colonel de la Pena. In 1821, when General Agustin de Inturbide issued his Plan of Iguala calling for an independent Mexican Empire, Salas enthusiastically embraced the cause. During the rebellion that arose after the Plan of Montano was issued in 1827, he fought in defence of President Guadalupe Victoria, and two years later he fought to repel the invasion of Spain's General Isidro Barradas at Tampico.

Realising that Mexico needed a strong leader to keep order, and on being promoted to lieutenant colonel in 1832, he supported Santa Anna as the President of Mexico. He commanded the Jimenez *Permanente* Battalion, acting as second-in-command of Romero's attacking column in the Alamo assault.

Colonel Juan Morales (1802–47) was born at Pueblo in Mexico. His first military service was as a cadet in the battalion de la Libertad, serving in Augustin de Interbide in the fight against the Spanish in 1821. He joined Santa Anna in his political rise and revolution against the Federalist Government. During the Texas Revolution he was a colonel of the largest units in General Joaquin Ramirez de Sesma's Vanguard Brigade. He led a column of men against Crockett's Tennessee Volunteers. He commanded the San Luis Potosi *Activo* Battalion, and was in charge of the combined *Cazadore* company assault column at the Alamo. His dress uniform coat has been preserved at the San Jacinto Museum of History.

Lieutenant Colonel Pedro y Ampudia Grimarest (1805–68) was born at Havana in Cuba. He was in command of the Mexican artillery during the siege of the Alamo, and was present during the assault.

Colonel Jose Enrique de la Pena (1807–40) was born at Jalisco. He trained as a mining engineer and entered the Mexican Navy in 1825 as a cadet first class. In 1828, with the title 'Lover of the Navy', he wrote a series of articles for *El Sol* newspaper that were critical of naval management. In the same year he was on his way to a naval assignment at Vera Cruz when he met Santa Anna and instead remained with the general. He may have participated in military actions against Spanish forces when they invaded Tampico in 1829. He contracted smallpox in 1830, and in 1831 he was commissioned by the navy to study mathematics in Mexico. When Santa Anna came to power in 1833, he was granted a commission as captain in a cavalry unit.

For several years he had requested to be assigned to a legation overseas, and in May 1833 he was offered a post in London. However, he disliked the climate and language in the British capital, so he requested a change to Paris, which was refused, so he withdrew his request and asked to become a part of the Federal Division of the President, which was granted in December 1833. A request to be assigned to the Mexican Legation in the United States in May 1834 was denied. At the onset of the Texas Revolution he had been demoted to lieutenant, and he was appointed as a staff officer for the elite *Zapadores* Battalion.

Brigadier General Juan Valentin Amador (1781–1851) was born in Cuba. He served in the Spanish Lancers until joining the Army of the Three Guarantees under Augustin de Iturbide. He was promoted to brigadier general in 1831. He led the first Mexican troops over the northern defences of the Alamo.

General Joaquín Ramírez y Sesma (1796–1839) was born in Mexico City. He commanded the vanguard of the Ejercito Operaciónes, and commanded cavalry in the Alamo.

Brigadier General Manuel Fernandez Castrillon (1780–1836) was a native of Cuba. He fought with Santa Anna in the defence of Vera Cruz, and became his aide-de-camp. He served with expert efficiency as second-in-command of Duque's assault column on the Alamo. A humane and honourable soldier, he often voiced his exception to some of Santa Anna's decisions, including the hurried assault, and he pleaded for clemency on behalf of some of the Alamo defenders. He would do the same for the captives who became victims of the Goliad massacre.

General Ventura Mora (born 1796) was a native of San Esteban Panuco, Tamualipas, Mexico. He held the rank of brevet-general, commanding the *Permanente* Dolores Cavalry Regiment.

Colonel Francisco Duque (1792–1854) was a native of Cocila in the Mexican state of Jalisco. He was promoted colonel in 1830. He commanded the Toluca *Activo* Battalion during the assault on the north ramparts in the battle of the Alamo, during which he was wounded in the leg.

Colonel Jose Vincente Minon (1802–78) was born at Cadiz in Spain in 1802, and joined the Mexican Independence movement, fighting at the battles of Arroyo Hondo and Azcapotzalco. He was second-in-command of Morales' *Cazadore* column in the Alamo assault.

Colonel Jose Maria Romero was 38 years of age at the time of the Texas Revolution. He commanded the Matamoros *Permanente* Battalion during the eastern attack column at the Alamo assault.

General Martin Perfecto de Cos was born at Vera Cruz in 1800, the son of an attorney. Becoming an army cadet at the age of 20, he served in the Fijo de Vera Cruz Regiment before joining the Army of the Three Guarantees under Augustin de Iturbide. He is believed to have been married to Lucinda López de Santa Anna, the general's sister. He was commander of the Eastern Internal Provinces, and had commanded Mexican forces in Texas from 18 September 1835. Captain Carey of the Texas artillery described him as 'a bold aspiring young general'. His orders were to collect taxes and deal with the agitation being provoked by colonists.

Lieutenant Francisco Narciso Castañeda Fernandez was born in October 1799 and was baptised in the parish church of San Juan Bautista de la Punta de Lampazos (now Lampazos de Naranjo), Nuevo León, on 1 November 1799. He was a son of Juan de Castañeda Quevedo and Josefa Fernández. His father served as an officer in the Compañías Volantes; a Spanish light cavalry unit used to patrol the northern provinces of New Spain. In June 1813, Francisco entered the Presidio service as a cadet in the same company as his father, following the Spanish practice of allowing teenage sons of officers to enter military service. In July 1818 he was promoted to *alferez* (2nd lieutenant) and transferred to the Second Compañía Volante of Tamaulipas in northeast Mexico, a detachment of which was stationed in Tejas. He was breveted to lieutenant in 1821, and in November 1823 he joined the La Segunda Compañía Volante de San Carlos de Parras (usually shortened to Álamo de Parras), a company of 100 Spanish lancers, which had been stationed in Tejas since 1803. The Alamo de Parras Company was stationed at the Villa de San Fernando, where Francisco was promoted to lieutenant in 1827. From there he took part in many of the skirmishes around the town against Indian raids and bandit activity.

3

THE SIEGE OF BEXAR

A unit of Mexican forces under General de Cos and Lieutenant Castaneda was landed at Matamoros on the eastern coast, and Cos was so concerned about the rising tensions in the region that on 5 July 1835 he prepared a declaration (a copy of which still exists), stating in both Spanish and English:

> The Brigadier General Martin Perfect de Cos, Commanding General and Inspector of the Eastern Internal States. In the Name of the President of the Republic: I make it known to all and every one of the inhabitants of the three departments of Texas, that whenever, under any pretext whatsoever, or through a badly conceived zeal in favour of the individuals who have acted as authorities in the state, and have been deposed by the resolution of the Sovereign General Congress, any should attempt to disturb the public order and peace, that the inevitable consequences of the war will bear upon them and their property, inasmuch as they do not wish to improve the advantages afforded them by their situation, which places them beyond the uncertainties that have agitated the people of the centre of the Republic.
>
> If the Mexican Government has cheerfully lavished upon the new settlers all its worthiness of regard, it will likewise know how to repress with strong arm all those who, forgetting their duties to the nation which has adopted them as their children, are pushing forward with a desire to live at their own option without any subjection to the laws. Wishing, therefore, to avoid the confusion which would result from the excitement of some bad citizens, I make the present declaration, with the resolution of entertaining it.

General Cos eventually moved his headquarters to San Antonio de Bejar, and the garrison numbered about 650 men. Realising the amount of hostility displayed against them all around the town, Cos fortified the plazas west of the San Antonio River and the Alamo. The Mexicans were gradually reinforced to over a thousand troops.

Gonzales was a settlement about 60 miles to the east of San Antonio. In 1831 the Mexicans provided the town with a bronze 6-pounder cannon, which they later mounted to serve as a visual deterrent to marauding hostile Comanche and Apache Indians.

In his 1874 biography of Crockett, John Abbott stated that when Crockett arrived there in 1836: 'It was a flourishing little Mexican town of about one thousand inhabitants, situated in a romantic dell, about sixty miles west of the River Sabine. The Mexicans and the Indians were very nearly on an intellectual and social equality. Groups of Indians, harmless and friendly, were ever sauntering through the streets of the little town.'

The incident that provoked hostilities that led to the outbreak of the Texas Revolution occurred at Gonzales. By 1835 the Mexican military in San Antonio had become concerned about the Texan attitude towards them and, suspecting that the cannon could be used against them, they requested for it to be returned, a condition on which it had been provided. On 1 October 1835, a troop of a hundred dragoons, under Lieutenant Castaneda, was sent out to retrieve it.

When the Mexicans got to Gonzales they found their path blocked by eighteen militiamen, later called the 'Old Eighteen', and having received instructions to avoid confrontation the Mexican troops were ordered to fall back. During the night the men of Gonzales crossed the river to confront the Mexicans, but it was foggy and impossible to fight, and they even bumped into each other, so both groups fell back to wait for first light. On the following day the Americans had increased to 180 men, and when the now outnumbered Mexicans tried to negotiate with the colonists the defiant Texans pointed to the gun and challenged the Mexicans to 'Come and take it'. The Texans rallied around the gun and resisted, forcing the Mexicans to withdraw, and with what are now considered to be the first shots fired during the Texas Revolution, the Texans caused some casualties including two soldiers killed.

Among the 'Old Eighteen' was Thomas J Jackson, who was born in Ireland in 1808. He left his native land and travelled to Missouri, where he married a local girl named Louise Cottle (1805–45) at St Charles in Missouri. They had three children, Margaret Jackson Brown (1828–92), who was born in Lincoln County, Missouri; George Washington (1829–52); who was born in Gonzales; and William, who was also born in 1829 and may have been George's twin. His wife was a sister of fellow Alamo defender George Washington Cottle.

The DeWitt Colony in Tejas land grant records show he entered the colony on 6 July 1829, with a family of four, and received a site of land. His league was south-east of Gonzales next to that of his father-in-law, Jonathan Cottle. On 18 September 1830, he registered his mark and cattle brand in Gonzales, which was witnessed by the Gonzales District Comisario: 'His ear mark a swallow fork in the right ear, and a half cross in the left ear, and his brand the letter T and J united which he says is his true mark and brand and that he has no other.'

The colonists were elated by their seemingly easy success and a Consultation Convention created a provisional government, which declared its intention to set up a Texas state. They began to recruit volunteers to form the Texan 'Army of the People', which soon grew to three hundred men, and elected Stephen Austin as its commander to try to bring some kind of unity to its ranks.

Newspapers in New Orleans for 26 November 1835 published the following letter received from one of the volunteers waiting to advance on Bexar:

> In Camp, Gonzales, 25 October – Dear Sir, the company of volunteers to which I belong is now in three days march of our main army, and we will leave tomorrow to join them; they are encamped six miles this side of San Antonio, and have been there six or eight days, waiting for reinforcements, which are duly coming in, and our cannon, to the number of five or six pieces, which will be here in six days. What is to be done? You will learn hereafter, now I am not able to inform you. I shall be in your city about the middle of November.
>
> San Antonio is garrisoned by a strong fortress commanding most of the town, and the streets barricaded and defended by cannon – cannon on the church, which is stone. Most of the houses are of stone, and occupied by the military, all the families having left. A number of Mexicans have joined our army. General Cos says he is ready for a fight.

On the same day as the letter was written, 25 October, in the last offensive sent out of San Antonio by General Cos, Mexican troops under the experienced Colonel Domingo Ugartechea (1794–1839) launched a surprise attack on a Texan unit under Colonel James Bowie camped near Mission Concepcion, not far from San Antonio. The attack was repulsed, and the Texans suffered two casualties, one being Captain Richard Andrews, the first soldier of the Texas army to be killed in action during the war. The Mexicans suffered several more casualties.

At a council of officers under Colonel Bowie's command, held to the south of Bexar on 2 November, Captain Thomas Parrott was one of only two men who favoured an immediate storming of the town, and voted against the division uniting with the main army.

On 26 November, Texan scout Erastus Deaf Smith, brought news that a Mexican pack train guarded by about a hundred Mexican soldiers was making for Bexar. The Texans, convinced that it was carrying silver to pay the Mexican garrison and buy supplies, decided to attack it. General Burleson ordered Colonel James Bowie to take about fifty mounted men to intercept it; and about 100 infantry followed. The train was approaching Bexar when General Cos witnessed the attack commence and he sent out reinforcements. The Texans repulsed several attacks by Mexican soldiers, who were forced to retreat back into Bexar. When the Texans examined the abandoned pack train they discovered that the mules carried freshly cut grass to feed the garrison's horses, and therefore the skirmish came to be known as 'the Grass Fight'. Four Texans were injured, and several Mexicans were killed.

Alexander Edwin Sweet remembered '... seeing in the old Campo Santo, of San Antonio, a pile of skulls, each one of which was bored by a rifle ball. These were the skulls of Mexicans who fell in what was known as "The Grass Fight" near that town.'

On 14 December 1835, William Ridgeway Carey had been elected captain by popular vote of the men of the Texan Artillery. Carey had joined the volunteer army of Texas and was among the troops that marched to Gonzales during the fight for the Gonzales cannon. His Artillery company, which he called his *Invincibles*, were to provide a large unit at Bexar and the Alamo. They appear to have been a tough group of men and he had great faith in their ability.

In a letter written to his family from San Antonio de Bexar on 12 January 1836, and mailed at Natchitoches on 7 February 1836, Captain Carey stated:

This place [Bexar and the Alamo] is an ancient Mexican fort and town divided by a small river which emanates from springs. The town has two squares and the church in the centre, one a military and the other a government square. The Alamo, or the fort as we call it, is a very old building built for the purpose of protecting the citizens from hostile Indians.

The Mexican army, or rather part of them, came to this place, commanded by Martin de Perfecto Cos, a bold aspiring young general. The town of Gonzales is about 78 miles below this place on the Guadalupe River. The enemy (as I shall now call them) sent about 200 of their troops to Gonzales after cannon that they sent there for the use of the citizens to fight the Indians. We then were aroused and watched closely their movements. Volunteers were called for to fight for their country. I was one of the first that started, about 150 of us ready in a moment's warning, and we marched to Gonzales and put the enemy to flight, and they retreated to this place.

We then considered it essentially necessary for the security of our peace to drive them from this place, but we concluded to wait for reinforcements as we were so few in number, and they in a fortified place, but unfortunately for us they commenced fortifying the town and strengthening the Alamo until it became almost impossible to overcome them. Our number increased gradually to the amount of 800, but on account of so many officer-seekers there was nothing but confusion, contention, and arid discord throughout the encampment, which was within half-a-mile of the place, for we came up to endeavour to starve them out, and on 4 December a retreat was ordered to the satisfaction of many, but to the grief of a few brave souls who were among the first that volunteered, and who preferred death in the cause rather than such a retreat.

Among his troops were five Irishmen. Robert Evans was born in Derry (Londonderry) Ireland, in 1804, and had travelled to New York in 1827 on *Atlantic*. He may have served in the British Army because he joined the American army as a major, which was a higher rank than would normally be given to a new recruit. Then he travelled by ship from New York to New Orleans, and then on to Texas, where he lived at San Antonio Ward 7 in Bexar. He was married to Eliza (formerly Porter), who had been born in England in 1798. After the siege of Bexar he served as master of ordnance of the Bexar garrison, being described as: 'black-haired, blue-eyed, nearly six feet tall and always merry'.

Major Evans' second in command at the Alamo was Captain Samuel Blair. According to the list of defenders put together not long after the fall of the Alamo by William Fairfax Gray, he was listed as Captain S.C. Blair of Ireland, but modern research has brought to light that he was actually born in Tennessee.

Sergeant William B. Ward was born in Ireland in 1806. He arrived in Texas by way of New Orleans. He achieved the rank of sergeant, but during his time in San Antonio he gained a reputation for being drunk, using bad language, and being generally unruly.

Burke Trammell was born in Ireland in 1810. He had travelled with his brother James from Tennessee to Texas, where they found a colony to apply for land grant of a third of a league. They settled in Bastrop colony sometime before 1835. The Texas Tax List places Burke in San Antonio in 1836. 'It is said that the Trammell brothers were among the first settlers of Bastrop or Travis colonies.' According to a certificate in the Texas Land Office he joined Carey's Artillery on 28 December 1835.

William Daniel Jackson was born in Ireland in 1807, being baptised at Clones in County Monaghan on 31 May 1807. He had worked as a sailor until the age of 24, when he sailed to America, arriving in New York aboard the brig *Calais Packet* on 8 March 1831. He moved to Kentucky, and was a major during the siege of Bexar.

Samuel E. Burns was born in Ireland in 1810 and was a resident of Natchitoches at the beginning of the Texas Revolution.

Sergeant William Daniel Hersee was born in England. I could not find anyone recorded with the middle name of Daniel. However, there was a William Hersee born to Charles and Jane Hersee, who was baptised at South Stoke, Arundel, in West Sussex, on 6 April 1806; and a William Hersee born to William and Mary Hersee, and baptised at Coldwaltham, Pulborough, in West Sussex, on 29 December 1808. He married Ann Maria (formerly French) on 22 April 1826, at Yapton near Bognor Regis in West Sussex, and they had four children. He took his family to America, and subsequently lived in New York, until moving to New Orleans. He is believed to have already held the rank of sergeant when he arrived in Texas in 1834. He is listed on the original muster roll as belonging to Captain Carey's Artillery Company. His name appears as a private in the New Orleans Greys on the Nacogdoches memorial, but he is not on the original muster roll.

Daniel Bourne was born at Woodchurch near Ashford in Kent, where much of the population worked as rural labourers. Findmypast records that Daniel Bourne was baptised at All Saints Church in Woodchurch, on 11 December 1814. He was the son of a labourer named George Bourne, and his wife, Elizabeth. The Mid-Kent marriage index records two marriages. George Bourne married Elizabeth Ditton, at All Saints Church in Maidstone on 10 April 1809; and another George Bourne married Elizabeth Hogbin, at Lydd, Romney Marsh, on 19 July 1812.

He and his brothers left their beautiful home village to travel to London to board the *Montreal*, and arrived at New York on 8 May 1835. They moved to DeWitt Colony and settled in Gonzales, where Daniel received a land grant as a single man. He took part in the siege of Bexar as a member of Captain Thomas F.L. Parrott's artillery company and joined Carey's artillery unit when they entered the Alamo. His brothers filed a claim as his heirs and in 1858 received a certificate for acreage in Pinto County, Texas.

Private James C. Gwynn was born in England. A James Gwynn was baptised on 1 August 1802, at Bridgnorth St Leonard in Shropshire, his parents being Charles and Hannah Gwynn; and a James Gwynn was baptised at Aldbourne in Wiltshire, on 2 January 1804. His parents were Thomas and Ann. I could not find a James Gwynn with the initial

C for a middle name, or with the surname spelt in any other way. He moved to Texas from Mississippi. He joined the Texas army and took part in the siege of Bexar. The heirs of James Gwinn were awarded 1476 acres of land at Milam in Burleston County, Texas.

Anthony Wolf was born of an English family on 17 February 1782, probably in Spain, and he may have been of Jewish extract, with the surname of Abraham. He apparently settled in the Louisiana-Texas territory prior to 1818. He gained a reputation for being skilled in working with indigenous American Indians, and he was employed as an Indian scout and interpreter, embarking on various expeditions to treat with native Indians such as acting as emissary to Wichita Indians on the Brazos River on 6 October 1822. He went by way of Nacogdoches in Texas with James Dill, who introduced him to Governor Jose Trespalacios. A month later he went with Jose Antonio Mexia on an expedition to treat with Cherokee Indians, being described as born and raised a Spanish subject. It is said that he worked with Lafitte, moving slaves to Louisiana to be sold to rich planters.

He had been a lieutenant in the Louisiana Militia before the Louisiana Purchase. He and his wife, Sarah, settled in Nacogdoches County, and he began farming. They had two sons named Benjamin (born in 1824), and Michael (born in 1825). Sarah died in 1835, and Anthony went through a long illness, from which he recuperated at the home of John Hall at Washington-on-the-Brazos. When he travelled to San Antonio he took his two sons with him.

Second Sergeant John McGregor was born on 1 December 1797, at Aberfeldy in the parish of Dull, Perthshire, Scotland. He and his father, Thomas, boarded *Capandra* at Oban in Argyll on 8 June 1808, arriving at Charlottetown on Prince Edward Island on 6 August 1808. He settled in Nacogdoches, and on 8 June 1835 he received a Mexican Land Grant of 640 acres in Henderson County. He had also been given a piece of land in Cherokee County, part of Burnett's Colony, on which he had been farming the land.

Fourth Sergeant Isaac Robinson was born in Scotland in 1808. He arrived in Texas by way of Louisiana. He filed for a land grant, which was awarded by Refugio Colony on 24 September 1834. He took part in the siege of Bexar and entered the Alamo as 4th Sergeant. He and fellow Scotsman, David L Wilson, signed the Goliad Declaration of Independence on 20 December 1835. In his 2003 book *Alamo Traces: New Evidence and New Conclusions* Thomas Ricks Lindley suggests that Isaac Robinson was killed by Indians in Bastrop County after the Alamo.

Early research concerning Lewis Johnson suggests that he was from Wales, and may have been with Captain Carey's artillery. However,

30

his file held by the Daughters of the Texas Revolution contains a letter from the Johnson family that states he was born in Virginia, and that his family is not from Wales, plus a history of his family showing it is based in Virginia.

Note: Civil registration in the United Kingdom did not commence until 1837, so birth certificates were not available for any of the British defenders. The closest equivalents are baptism records, which at least provide details of the parents' names. Children were usually baptised within a few weeks of birth, and sometimes the date of birth was also recorded, although this varied by parish and whether the vicar thought it important to record the information or not.

***

A New Orleans arcade owner named Thomas Banks advocated that Texas should break from Mexico, and his red-brick building on Magazine Street was often used for meetings in the service of Texas independence. Consequently – according to 'A Campaign in Texas' published in *Blackwood's Edinburgh Magazine* for January 1846, taken from *Journeys and Fates of a German in Texas* by Herman Vollrath Ehrenburg – there appeared on posters 'in letters a foot high' at the corner of every street in New Orleans on the morning of 11 October 1835:

> A meeting of citizens this evening in the Arcade coffee house. It concerns the freedom and sovereignty of a people in whose veins the blood of the Anglo-Saxon flows. Texas, the prairieland, has risen in arms against the tyrant Santa Anna, and the greedy despotism of the Romish priesthood, and implores the assistance of the citizens of the Union. We have therefore convoked an assembly of the inhabitants of this city, and trust to see it numerously attended. *The Committee of Texas.*

Blackwood's Magazine continued the story:

> The summons of the Texian committee of New Orleans to their fellow citizens was enthusiastically responded to. At the appointed hour, the immense Arcade Coffeehouse was thronged to the roof, speeches in favour of Texian liberty were made and applauded to the echo; and two lists were opened – one for subscriptions, the other for the names of those who were willing to lend the aid of their arms to their oppressed fellow-countrymen. Before the meeting separated, ten thousand dollars were subscribed, and on the following afternoon, the steamer *Washita* ascended the Mississippi with the first company of volunteers. These had ransacked the tailors' shops for grey clothing, such being the colour best suited to the prairie, and thence they received the name of

31

'The Greys'; their arms were rifles, pistols, and the far-famed bowie-knife. The day after their departure, a second company of Greys set sail, but went round by sea to the Texian coast; and the third instalment of these ready volunteers was the company of Tampico Blues, who took ship for the port of Tampico.

The three companies consisted of Americans, English, French, and several Germans. Six of the latter nation were to be found in the ranks of the Greys; and one of them, a Prussian, of the name of Ehrenberg, who appears to have been for some time an inhabitant of the United States, and to be well acquainted with the country, its people, their language and peculiarities.

One of the Irish contingent was Captain Thomas William Ward (1807–72), who helped in the organisation of the Greys. He had been born in Dublin, to Henry Ward and his wife, who were English landowners. He had travelled to Quebec with them, and then on to New Orleans, where he studied engineering and architecture.

The Nacogdoches alcalde (mayor and Justice of the Peace), Adolphus Sterne, was present at the meeting and offered to supply weapons to the first fifty men who would volunteer for Texas. Over a hundred men appear to have been recruited, although no original full muster role exists. Sterne kept his word and on 3 November he entertained forty-five men with a 'Feast of Liberty' in his orchard at the front of his house. Two companies of militia volunteers were formed; the first under Captain Thomas H Breece, and the second under Captain Robert C Morris, and they took the title the New Orleans Grays (Greys). William Blazeby was appointed 2nd lieutenant in Captain Breece's 1st Company.

Unlike the majority of the Texan volunteers, the Grays looked like soldiers, with uniforms, well-maintained rifles, adequate ammunition, and some semblance of discipline. A circular printed in Nacogdoches said the men of Breece's company were 'mostly athletic mechanics, who have abandoned their homes and lucrative employments for the disinterested purpose of sustaining the righteous cause of freedom. Their very appearance must convince every Texan that they will either "do or die".'

Weapons and equipment were probably provided from the stores of the Washington Guards, whose armoury was on the second floor of the arcade. Morris's company possibly carried rifles, and Breece's men were issued with United States-pattern muskets. They also carried swords and large knives. They took their name from the colour of their uniforms and a member of Morris's company stated that 'the colour of our uniform was a grey jacket and pants with a seal-skin cap'. Indians around Nacogdoches sometimes mistook them for United States Army regulars.

Adolphus Sterne stated: 'The appearance of the Grays at Nacogdoches on their way to San Antonio had a fine effect on the Cherokee Indians, a large number of whom were then in town. Their fine uniform caps and coats attracted the notice of the chief, Bolles. He inquired if they were Jackson's men?'

'Certainly they are,' said Sterne.

'Are there more coming?'

'Yes,' was the reply.

'How many more?' asked Bolles.

'Count the hairs on your head and you will know.'

In twenty minutes the Indians had all left the town.

Blackwood's Magazine reported:

Great was the enthusiasm, and joyful the welcome, with which the Texian colonists received the first company of volunteers, when, under the command of Captain Breece, they landed from their steamboat upon the southern bank of the river Sabine. No sooner had they set foot on shore, than a flag of blue silk, embroidered with the words, 'To the first company of Texian volunteers from New Orleans', was presented to them in the name of the women of Texas; the qualification of Texian citizens was conferred upon them; every house was placed at their disposal for quarters; and banquets innumerable were prepared in their honour.

But the moment was critical – time was too precious to be expended in feasts and merry-making, and they pressed onwards. A two days' march brought them to San Augustin, two more to Nacogdoches, and thence, after a short pause, they set out on their journey of five hundred miles to St Antonio, where they expected first to burn powder. Nor were they deceived in their expectations. They found the Texian militia encamped before the town, which, as well as its adjacent fort of the Alamo, was held by the Mexicans, the Texians were besieging it in the best manner their imperfect means and small numbers would permit.

The two units had actually left New Orleans to join the Texas army within two days of each other. Morris's 2nd Company of seventy men set off first. Morris was promoted to major and assumed command of a division made up of both companies of Grays, and Captain William Cooke took over command of his old unit. Breece's fifty-man 1st Company took an overland route up the Mississippi and Red rivers aboard the steamer *Washita*. They disembarked at Alexandria and followed the Old Spanish Trail to its crossing into Texas at Gaines Ferry. At San Augustine a delegation of local Texas women presented the company with the standard that the Greys adopted as their flag. It is a guidon made of a blue silk banner displaying an eagle and sunburst with the inscription FIRST COMPANY OF TEXAN VOLUNTEERS! FROM NEW ORLEANS. The eagle carries a banner in its beak with the motto: 'GOD and LIBERTY'. They were welcomed with a public dinner at San Augustine and at Nacogdoches they were treated to a dinner of roasted bear and champagne. About thirty-five of the company were provided with horses before proceeding to San Antonio, where they arrived on 8 November 1835.

A detailed plaque dedicated to Captain Breece's Company of New Orleans Grays in Nacogdoches includes the names of fifteen British-born men who joined the unit. It is attached to a boulder on the northern edge of the parking lot at the Adolphus Sterne House, which is now a museum. Around the flag of the New Orleans Grays it states:

THE NEW ORLEANS GRAYS
CAPTAIN BREECE'S COMPANY IN NACOGDOCHES

Between recruitment in New Orleans on October 13 1835, and the Palm Sunday Massacre at Goliad – during 157 days of the Texas Revolution – 120 men of the two companies of New Orleans Grays fought at Bexar; and units of the Grays fought at the Alamo, San Patricio, Agua Dulce, Refugio, Coleto and Goliad. The massacre at Goliad was the end of the Grays as a military force, but seven of the original 120 Grays survived these battles to fight at San Jacinto.

Alphonsus Sterne of Nacogdoches recruited, outfitted, and on November 3 1835, he entertained 45 men of Captain Thomas Breece's First Company of the New Orleans Grays with a 'Feast of Liberty' in his orchard in front of his house. The next day, Captain Breece's Grays rode off on horses furnished by Sterne and the citizens of Nacogdoches to fight in the battle of Bexar. In the following bloody days of the Texas Revolution, twenty-five of Breece's Grays died at the Alamo and eight at Goliad. One survived to fight at San Jacinto.

Nacogdoches pays tribute to Captain Thomas H. Breece's Company of New Orleans Grays and honors them for their service and for the sacrifices they made fighting for what became the Republic of Texas. Nacogdoches thanks the Grays for honouring this town with their presence on their way to the battlefield, death, and Texas history.

Capt Thomas H Breece (Louisiana) survived
1st Lt John Baugh (Virginia) died at the Alamo
1st Lt George Main (Virginia) died at the Alamo
*2nd Lt William Blazeby (Great Britain) died at the Alamo
Sgt George Andrews (?) died at the Alamo
Sgt John Jones (New York) died at the Alamo

Sgt Bennett McNelly (Pennsylvania) fought at San Jacinto
Sgt Robert Musselman (Pennsylvania) died at the Alamo
Pvt John Bright (North Carolina) joined the Matamoros expedition
Pvt John Casey (Ireland) expelled
Pvt Charles Clarke (Louisiana) died at Goliad
Pvt John Coffee (Ireland) expelled
Pvt John Cook (Great Britain) died at Bexar
Pvt Henry Cortman (Germany) died at the Alamo
Pvt Robert Crossman (Pennsylvania) died at the Alamo
Pvt Stephen Dennison (Great Britain) died at the Alamo
Pvt Blaz Philippe Despellier (Louisiana) furloughed after Bexar
Pvt James R Dimpkins (Great Britain) died at the Alamo
Pvt Herbert Ehrenberg (Germany) escaped massacre at Goliad
Pvt Conrad Eigenaeur (Germany) died in the battle of Coleto
Pvt James Fitzgerald (Louisiana) deserted
Pvt James Girard Garrett (Louisiana) died at the Alamo
Pvt William Jones Gatlin (Tennessee) died at Goliad
Pvt Peter Griffin (Louisiana) spared at Goliad
*Pvt Daniel Hersee (Great Britain) died at the Alamo
Pvt Samuel Holloway (Tennessee) died at the Alamo
Pvt William D Howell (New York) died at the Alamo
Pvt T P Hutchinson (Tennessee) died at the Alamo
Pvt Thomas Kemp (Great Britain) escaped massacre at Goliad
Pvt William Linn (Boston) died at the Alamo
Pvt John McGee (Ireland) died at the Alamo
Pvt William Marshall (Tennessee) died at the Alamo
Pvt Peter Mattern (Germany) died at Goliad
Pvt Robert B Moore (Kentucky) died at the Alamo
Pvt John Mormon (Ireland) died at the Alamo
Pvt George Nelson (South Carolina) died at the Alamo
Pvt William Ross (Louisiana) expelled
Pvt John Scott (Pennsylvania) died at Goliad
Pvt John Shaw (Great Britain) deserted
Pvt Joseph H Spohn (Louisiana) spared at Goliad
Pvt John Spratt (Ireland) died at the Alamo
*Pvt Richard Starr (Great Britain) died at the Alamo
Pvt William Stephens (?) died at Goliad
*Pvt Henry Thomas (Great Britain) died at the Alamo
*Pvt Thomas Waters (Great Britain) died at the Alamo
Pvt Stephen Winship (New York) died at Goliad
Pvt W B Wood (New Jersey) died at Goliad

British notes – William Blazeby was a captain in the Alamo. Richard Starr is named Robert on the muster rolls for Bexar. Daniel Hersee is also listed on the muster roll for Captain Carey's Artillery; and Thomas

Waters transferred to the artillery when he entered the Alamo as a sergeant. Henry Thomas is believed to have been a German.

William Blazeby was born at Ipswich in Suffolk in 1795, the second child and oldest son of William Blazeby (1764–1836), and his wife, Frances (formerly Robinson, 1770–1838). Both his parents lived all their lives in Ipswich. William had seven siblings; all born in Ipswich – Susan (born in 1787); Robert (1800–76); Mary (born in 1803); Isaac (born in 1806); Thomas (1809–72); Charles (1813–56); and James (1816–80). William sailed to New York before moving south-west to New Orleans to seek his fortune. According to the *New Orleans Advertiser* for 28 March 1836, 'Three young men from our office, we learn, are among the slain. The names of William Blazeby and Robert Moore have been mentioned, that of the other we could not ascertain.'

Robert B. Moore was a 55-year-old Virginian, his parents having sailed from Ireland with the original name of O'Moore. Having moved to New Orleans, Robert joined Captain Thomas Breece's Company, and served under Captain Blazeby. His name appears on the New Orleans Grays Memorial as being a native of Kentucky. Another Alamo victim, Willis A. Moore, was his younger cousin. He was the second-oldest defender of the Alamo, the oldest being 56-year-old Corporal Gordon C. Jennings of Carey's Artillery Company.

Private John Cook was born in Britain, and was killed in action during the battle of Bexar.

Private Stephen Denison was born in England. The only man who fits his description in British records is Stephen Charles Denison, who was born to John and Charlotte Denison, and was baptised at St Marylebone in London, on 29 July 1811. He sailed to America from England on the ship *Industry*. He was a glazer and painter by trade. He travelled to Texas with Captain Breece's unit before he transferred to Captain Blazeby. On 4 November 1859, his heirs received a Donation Certificate for 640 acres of land in Crockett County, on the waters of the Devil's River, a tributary of the San Antonio River; and a Bounty Warrant of 320 acres of land, both for his service at Bexar.

Sergeant James R. Dimpkins was born in England in about 1804. He travelled to Texas with Captain Breece's unit before he transferred to Captain Blazeby's company.

John James McGee, John Morman and John Spratt were born in Ireland.

James Nowlan was born in England in 1809. He sailed to America with the intention to settle in San Antonio de Bexar. However, New Orleans was the closest port for a larger ship to discharge passengers. He then learned of the imminent revolution in Texas from the New

Orleans Grays, so he enlisted with Captain William Gordon Cooke's unit. He was severely wounded during the Siege of Bexar, and entered the Alamo with Captain Blazeby's company.

Richard (or Robert) Starr was born in England. The two main candidates for him in British records are Robert Starr, a son of Robert and Catherine Starr, who was baptised at Stepney in London, on 17 February 1811; and Richard Benjamin Starr, who was born on 2 March 1813, to a smithy named John Starr, and his wife, Mary Ann, and he was baptised on 20 March 1814. Their address was 50 High Street, St Paul, Shadwell, in the London Docklands area. He travelled to Texas as a member of Captain Breece's unit.

Although the plaque at Nacogdoches states that Henry Thomas came from Great Britain, it seems he was born in Germany in 1811.

Thomas Waters was born in England in 1812. He moved to Texas by way of New Orleans. He took part in the Siege of Bexar as a member of Captain Thomas Breece's Company of New Orleans Greys, and then transferred to Captain Carey's Artillery.

***

The Mexican army were in fact the first troops to be besieged during the Texas Revolution. They had fortified San Antonio's plazas, and after five days of fighting and being driven back building by building, General Cos sought to concentrate his troops at the Alamo.

Blackwood's Edinburgh Magazine published an account by an unknown participant of an incident that occurred while the Mexicans were in the Alamo complex, which stated:

> Towards nine o'clock a party crossed the field between our camp and the town, to reinforce a small redoubt erected by Cook's Grays, and provided with two cannon, which were continually thundering against the Alamo, and from time to time, knocking down a fragment of wall. The whole affair seemed like a party of pleasure, and every telling shot was hailed with shouts of applause. Meanwhile the enemy were not idle, but kept up a fire from eight or nine pieces, directed against the redoubt, the balls and canister ploughing up the ground in every direction, and driving clouds of dust towards the camp. It was no joke to get over the 600 or 800 yards that intervened between the latter and the redoubt, for there was scarcely any cover, and the Mexican artillery was far better served than ours.
>
> Nevertheless, the desire to have a full view of the Alamo, which, from the redoubt, presented an imposing appearance, induced eight men, including myself, to take a start across the field. It seemed as if the enemy had pointed at us every gun in the fort. The bullets fell around us

like hail, and, for a moment, the blasting tempest compelled us to take refuge behind a pecan tree. Here we stared at each other, and laughed heartily at the figure we cut, standing, eight men deep, behind a nut tree, whilst our comrades, both in the camp and the redoubt, shouted with laughter at every discharge that rattled amongst the branches over our heads.

'This is what you call making war,' said one of the party, Thomas Camp by name.

'And that,' said another, as a whole swarm of iron mosquitoes buzzed by him, 'is what we Americans call variations on Yankee Doodle.'

Just then there was a tremendous crash amongst the branches, and we dashed out from cover, and across to the redoubt only just in time, for the next moment the ground on which we had been standing was strewed with the heavy branches of the pecan tree. All was life and bustle in the little redoubt; the men were standing round the guns, talking and joking, and taking it by turns to have a shot at the old walls. Before firing, each man was compelled to name his mark, and say what part of the Alamo he meant to demolish, and then bets were made as to his success or failure.

'A hundred rifle bullets to twenty,' cried one man, 'that I hit between the third and fourth window of the barracks.'

'Done!' cried half-a-dozen voices. The shot was fired, and the clumsy artilleryman had to cast bullets all the next day.

'My pistols, the best in camp, by the by,' exclaimed another aspirant, 'against the worst in the redoubt.'

'Well, sir, I reckon I may venture,' said a hard-featured back-woodsman, in a green hunting shirt, whose pistols, if not quite so good as he'd wagered, were, at any rate, the next best.

Away drew the ball, and the pistols of the unlucky marksman were transferred to green-shirt, who generously drew forth his own, and handed them to the loser.

'Well, comrade, s'pose I must give you yer revenge. If I don't hit, you'll have your pistols back again.'

The cannon was loaded, and backwoodsman squinted along it, as if it had been his own rifle, his features twisted up into a mathematical calculation, and his right hand describing in the air all manner of geometrical figures. At last he was ready. One more squint along the gun, the match was applied, and the explosion took place. The rattle of the stones warned us that the ball had taken effect. When the smoke cleared away, we looked in vain for the third and fourth windows, and a tremendous hurrah burst forth for old Deaf Smith, as he was called for the bravest Texian who ever hunted across a prairie who subsequently, with a small corps of observation, did such good service on the Mexican frontier between Noches and the Rio Grande.

The restless and impetuous Yankee volunteers were not long in finding opportunities of distinction. Some Mexican sharpshooters having come down to the opposite side of the river, whence they fired into the redoubt, were repelled by a handful of the Greys, who then, carried away by their enthusiasm, drove in the enemy's outposts, and entered the suburbs of the town. They got too far, and were in imminent risk of being overpowered by superior numbers, when Deaf Smith came to their rescue with a party of their comrades.

Several days passed away in skirmishing, without any decisive assault being made upon the town or fort. The majority of the men were for attacking; but some of the leaders opposed it, and wished to retire into winter quarters in rear of the Guadalupe River, wait for further reinforcements from the States, and then, in the spring, again advance, and carry St Antonio by a *coup de main*. To an army, in whose ranks subordination and discipline were scarcely known, and where every man thought his opinion as worthy to be listened to as that of the general, a difference of opinion was destruction. The Texian militia, disgusted with their leader, Burleson, retreated in straggling parties across the Guadalupe; about four hundred men, consisting chiefly of the volunteers from New Orleans and the Mississippi, remained behind, besieging St Antonio, of which the garrison was nearly two thousand strong. The four hundred melted away, little by little, to two hundred and ten; but these held good, and resolved to attack the town. They did so, and took it, house by house, with small loss to themselves, and a heavy one to the Mexicans. On the sixth day, the garrison of the Alamo, which was commanded by General Cos, and which the deadly Texian rifles had reduced to little more than half its original numbers, capitulated. After laying down their arms, they were allowed to retire beyond the Rio Grande. Forty-eight pieces of cannon, four thousand muskets, and a quantity of military stores, fell into the hands of the Texians, whose total loss amounted to six men dead, and twenty-nine wounded.

Born in New York in 1787, Erastus 'Deaf' Smith suffered hearing loss at an early age. During the siege of Bexar he guided Colonel Francis White Johnson's column into the town. On 7 December 1835 he was wounded on the top of the Veramendi Palace at about the same time as Ben Milam was killed. When he recovered he served as a messenger for Colonel Travis, who considered him to be 'the bravest of the brave' and carried his letter from the Alamo on 15 February 1836. He fought in the battle of San Jacinto, led a company of Texas Rangers, and died in Richmond in 1837.

After several weeks of siege tactics the final assault on Bexar began on Saturday, 5 December 1835. Early that morning James C Neill distracted the Mexican forces with artillery fire on the Alamo before dawn. As the artillery boomed, two divisions launched surprise attacks. Colonel Francis Johnson led his men southward along the San

Antonio River into what is now Soledad Street towards the Veramendi Palace and Garza house on each side of the street north of the plaza, while Colonel Benjamin Rush Milam led his force further west and then southward down Main Street. The Texans could draw confidence from the greater accuracy of their rifles, and their superior skill in using them.

The editor of *Texas Siftings* confirmed: 'The extraordinary number of Mexicans killed in all the engagements of the Texas revolution is explained by the fact that the Texans were mostly from Kentucky and Tennessee; men who could bark squirrels with a rifle all day long. Such marksmen rarely missed as large a target as a Mexican. In fact, almost all the Mexicans killed in these fights were shot through the head.'

Cannon and musket fire from Mexican soldiers mainly of the Morelos *Permanente* Battalion positioned in trees, the church tower and some of the buildings prevented the Texans from advancing during the day and silenced one of their cannon. Lieutenant Blazeby's company took an active part in the capture of the Veramendi Palace, during which time Private John Cook was killed and Sergeant William Daniel Hersee and Private James McGee were wounded. They proceeded to fortify the house, digging trenches and building earthworks.

At a meeting held in the courtyard of the Veramendi House on Monday, 7 December, Ben Milam was not aware that a Morelos *cazadore* marksman named Felix de la Garza had his rifle trained on him. A shot rang out and Milam fell dead with a bullet in his head. The sniper was killed soon afterwards.

Captain Ward had followed Milam, and he was serving at the head of an artillery unit when he had his leg blown away by a cannonball at about the same time. It has been suggested that Milam's body and Ward's leg were buried in the same grave. He returned to New Orleans to have a false limb fitted, and soon came to be known as 'Peg-Leg Ward'.

On Tuesday, 8 December Cooke led a party of his men against the Priest's House on the main plaza. Six of his men were severely wounded, including Private James Nowlan. It is not known if the wounds prevented any of them from taking an active part in the fighting in the Alamo, but it seems that the injuries were serious.

Four companies of Cos's cavalry rode away rather than continue the struggle and consequently on Wednesday, 9 December Cos sent a white flag to General Edward Burleson. After two days of negotiations the Texan commander accepted the surrender of most Mexican equipment and weapons but he allowed Cos and his 1,100 men to retire southward. Texan casualties numbered about thirty rifles, while

Mexican losses, primarily in the Morelos *Permanente* Battalion, which defended San Antonio, totalled about 150.

Captain Carey recorded:

> We rallied around a brave soul (Colonel Milam) and requested him to be our leader. He consented, and 150 of us declared to take the place or die in the attempt; while a large number of them endeavoured to discourage us and said we would all be butchered. But a few more saw we were resolute and joined, until our number was 220.
>
> On the next morning, about day-break, we marched in the town under the heavy fire of their cannon and musketry, but we succeeded in getting possession of some stone houses (which were outside the square) that sheltered us a little from their fires until we could make breastwork for ourselves. We laboured hard day and night for five days, still gaining possession, when on the morning of the fifth day they sent in a flag of truce to the extreme joy of all of us. Thus a handful of Militia of 220 in number stormed a strongly-fortified place, which was supported with two thousand citizens and soldiers (of the enemy).
>
> Here I must remark, on the third day of the siege our leader fell in the battle. Another usurped the command; who never was in favour of storming, and had ordered the retreat, but he was in time to make a disgraceful treaty. Some strongly suspect bribery was the cause, but whether or ignorance I cannot decide.
>
> The enemy, on the third day of the siege, raised a black flag (which says no quarter), and when we had whipped them by washing the flag with the blood of about 300 of them we would have to make a treaty and not a child's bargain. However, it is done now, and it's too late to alter until we have another fight, which we expect shortly.

The following despatch of 6 December 1835 was sent by Ben Milam and Edward Burleson, to the provisional government at San Filipe:

> Yesterday morning, at daylight, or rather some twenty minutes before, Colonel Milam, with a party of about 300 volunteers, made an assault upon the town of Bexar. His party he distributed in two divisions, which, on entering the town, took possession of two buildings near each other – near the place where they have been ever since battling with the enemy. They have so far had a fierce contest, the enemy offering a strong and obstinate resistance. The houses occupied by us command some of the cannon in the place, or have silenced them entirely, as it is reported to us. The issue is doubtful, of course.
>
> Ugartechea is on the way, with considerable reinforcements; how near has not yet been exactly ascertained; but certainly he is not more than from fifty to sixty miles off. This express has been despatched

for an immediate supply of ammunition, as much powder and lead as can possibly be sent instantly. Of the first-mentioned article, there is none beyond the cannon cartridges already made up. I hope that good mules, or horses, will be procured to send on these articles with the greatest possible speed, travelling night and day, for there is not a moment to be lost. Reinforcements of men are, perhaps, indispensable to our salvation. I hope every exertion will be made to force them to our relief immediately.

In his official report of the storming of San Antonio, Colonel Johnson says:

At seven o'clock a heavy cannonading from the town was seconded by a well-directed fire from the Alamo, which for a time prevented the possibility of covering our lines, or effecting a safe communication between the two divisions. In consequence of the twelve-pounder having been dismounted, and want of proper cover for the other gun, little execution was done by our artillery during the day. We were, therefore, reduced to a close and well-directed fire from our rifles, which, notwithstanding the advantageous position of the enemy, obliged them to slacken their fire, and several times to abandon their artillery within range of our shot. Our loss during the day was one private killed; one colonel and one first-lieutenant severely wounded; one colonel slightly, three privates dangerously, six severely, and three slightly. During the whole of the night (of the 5th) the two divisions were occupied in strengthening their positions, opening trenches, and effecting a safe communication, although exposed to a heavy cross-fire from the enemy, which slackened towards morning. I may remark that want of proper tools rendered this undertaking doubly arduous.

At daylight of the 6th the enemy were observed to have occupied the tops of the houses in our front, where, under cover of breastworks, they opened through loop-holes a very brisk fire of small arms on our whole line, followed by a steady cannonading from the town, in front, and from the Alamo on the left flank, with few interruptions during the day. A detachment of Captain Crane's company, under Lieutenant W V McDonald, followed by others, gallantly possessed themselves, under a severe fire, of the house to the right, and in advance of the first division, which considerably extended our line; while the rest of the army was occupied in returning the enemy's fire and strengthening our trenches, which enabled our artillery to do some execution, and complete a safe communication from right to left. Our loss this day amounted to three privates severely wounded and two slightly. During the night the fire from the enemy was inconsiderable, and our people were occupied in making and filling sand-bags, and otherwise strengthening our lines.

At daylight on the 7th it was discovered that the enemy had, during the night previous, opened a trench on the Alamo side of the river, and on the left flank. The late Thomas W. Ward lost a leg here, and was afterwards nick-named Old Peg-Leg. Hon. Sam A. Maverick and J.W. Smith did good service in this storming party, as well as strengthened their battery on the cross street leading to the Alamo. From the first, they [the Mexicans] opened a brisk fire of small arms; from the last, a heavy cannonade, as well as small arms, which was kept up until eleven o'clock, when they were silenced by our superior fire. [This seems to be the Deaf Smith action described earlier from *Blackwood's Magazine*.]

About twelve o'clock, Henry Karnes, of Captain York's company, exposed to a heavy fire from the enemy, gallantly advanced to a house in front of the first division; and, with a crow-bar, forced an entrance, through which the whole company immediately followed him, and made a secure lodgement. In the evening, the enemy renewed a heavy fire from all the directions.

... at about half-past three o'clock, as our gallant commander, Colonel Milam, was passing into the yard of my position (the house of Veramendi) he received a rifle shot in the head, which caused his instant death – an irreparable loss at so critical a moment. Our casualties otherwise, during the day, were only two privates slightly wounded.

At a meeting of officers, held at seven o'clock, I was invested with the chief command, with Major Morris as my second. Captains Llewellyn, English, Crane, and Landrum, with their respective companies, forced their way into, and took possession of the house of Don J. Antonio Navarro, an advanced and important position close to the square. The fire of the enemy became interrupted and slack during the whole night, and the weather exceedingly cold and wet.

The morning of the 8th continued cold and wet, and but little firing on either side. At nine o'clock, the same companies who took possession of Don J. Antonio Navarro's house, aided by a detachment of the Grays, advanced and occupied the Zambrano Row, leading to the Square, without any accident. The brave conduct on this occasion of William Graham, of Cook's company of Grays, merits mention. A heavy fire of artillery and small arms was opened on this position by the enemy, who disputed every inch of ground, and after suffering a severe loss in officers and men, were obliged to retire from room to room, until they evacuated the whole building. During this time, our men were reinforced by a detachment from York's company, under the command of Lieutenant Gill. The cannonading was exceedingly heavy from all quarters during the day, but did no essential damage. Our loss consisted of one captain seriously wounded and two privates severely.

At seven o'clock pm, the party in Zambrano's Row were reinforced by Captains Swisher, Alley, Edwards, and Duncan, and their respective companies.

This evening we had undoubted information of the arrival of a strong reinforcement to the enemy, under Colonel Ugartechea. At half-past ten o'clock pm, Captains Cook and Patton, with the company of New Orleans Grays and a company of Brazoria Volunteers, forced their way into the priest's house in the square, although exposed to the fire of a battery. Before this, however, the division was reinforced from the reserve by Captains Cheshire, Lewis, and Sutherland, and their companies.

Immediately after we got possession of the priest's house, the enemy opened a furious cannonade from all their batteries, accompanied by incessant volleys of small arms, against every house in our possession, and every part of our lines, which continued unceasingly until half-past six o'clock, am, of the 9th, when they sent a flag of truce, with an intimation that they desired to capitulate. Our loss in this night's attack, consisted of one man only, dangerously wounded, while in the act of spiking a cannon.

On the morning of the 10th, General Cos surrendered, and on the 14th set out for the Rio Grande, with 1,105 troops, the remainder of his army, which amounted to about 1,400, having concluded to remain in San Antonio. Thus by the heroism of Milam and his comrades was the stronghold of the Mexicans in Texas taken, but at the loss of that gallant soldier, the brave Milam.

Often have I entered the Old Veramandi and asked: 'Where is Milam's grave?' But no one ever answered the question, and unless some of his comrades in this brilliant achievement shall return to the place of his glory, and mark the grave where our hero lay buried, it will be unknown to future generations.

The statement of Capitulation was presented to General Cos on Sunday, 11 December 1835, believed to have been at a house which still exists on La Vallita Street, which was:

Entered into by General Martin Perfecto de Cos, of the Permanent troops, and General Edward Burleson, of the Colonial troops of Texas, being desirous of preventing the further effusion of blood, and the ravages of civil war, have agreed on the following stipulations:

1. That general Cos and his officers retire into the interior of the republic, under parole of honor; that they will not in any way oppose the re-establishment of the federal Constitution of 1824.
2. That the one hundred infantry lately arrived with the convicts, the remnant of the battalion of Morelos, and the cavalry, retire with the general; taking their arms and ten rounds of cartridges for their muskets.
3. That the general take the convicts brought in by Colonel Ugartechea, beyond the Rio Grande.

4. That it is discretionary with the troops to follow their general, remain, or go to such point as they may deem proper: but in case they should all or any of them separate, they are to have their arms, &c.
5. That all the public property, money, arms and munitions of war, be inventoried and delivered to general Burleson.
6. That all private property be restored to its proper owners.
7. That three officers of each army be appointed to make out the inventory, and see that the terms of the capitulation be carried into effect.
8. That three officers on the part of General Cos remain for the purpose of delivering over the said property, stores, &c.
9. That General Cos with his force, for the present, occupy the Alamo; and general Burleson, with his force, occupy the town of Bejar; and that the soldiers of neither party pass to the other, armed.
10. General Cos shall, within six days from the date hereof, remove his force from the garrison he now occupies.
11. In addition to the arms before mentioned, General Cos shall be permitted to take with his force, a four-pounder, and ten rounds of powder and ball.
12. The officers appointed to make the inventory and delivery of the stores, &c. shall enter upon the duties to which they have been appointed, forthwith.
13. The citizens shall be protected in their persons and property.
14. General Burleson will furnish General Cos with such provisions as can be obtained, necessary for his troops to the Rio Grande, at the ordinary price of the country.
15. The sick and wounded of General Cos's army, together with a surgeon and attendants, are permitted to remain.
16. No person, either citizen or soldier, to be molested on account of his political opinions hitherto expressed.
17. That duplicates of this capitulation be made out in Castilian and English, and signed by the commissioners appointed, and ratified by the commanders of both armies.
18. The prisoners of both armies, up to this day, shall be put at liberty.

The commissioners, Jose Juan Sanchez, adjutant inspector; Don Ramon Musquiz, and lieutenant Francisco Rada, and interpreter, Don Miguel Arciniega; appointed by the commandant and inspector, General Martin Perfecto de Cos, in connection with Colonel F. W. Johnson, Major R. C. Morris, and Captain J. G. Swisher, and interpreter John Cameron; appointed on the part of general Edward Burleson: after a long and serious discussion, adopted the eighteen preceding articles, reserving their ratification by the generals of both armies. In virtue of which, we have signed this instrument in the city of Bejar, on the 11th of December, 1835.

The notorious 'Tornell Decree', which was written on 30 December 1835, and was published in Texas and New Orleans soon after that date, stated that all foreigners who took up arms against the Mexican government would be deemed a pirate and dealt with as such; which practically gave Santa Anna a free licence to execute all prisoners.

Colonel de la Pena's opinion was: 'When in this or some other discussion the subject of what to do with prisoners was brought up in case the enemy surrendered before the assault, the example of Arredondo was cited; during the Spanish rule he had hanged eight hundred or more colonists after triumphing in a military action, and this conduct was taken as a model. General Castrillon and Colonel Almonte then voiced principles regarding the rights of men, philosophical and humane principles that did them honour, but their arguments were fruitless.'

Note: General Jose Joaquin de Arredondo (1768–1837) was a Spanish-born military commander of Tejas, who is remembered in Texas history as a butcher because of the incident referred to by Colonel de la Pena, which occurred on 18 August 1815 after the battle of Medina, fought about 20 miles south of San Antonio de Bexar; and is considered to have been the bloodiest battle in Texas history.

***

The situation for the Texans was made worse by the fact that they were constantly having trouble with marauding Comanche raiding parties, and on 8 January 1836 Colonel Neill sent Governor Smith and the Texas Council a message stating, 'We have this morning received an ambassador from the Comanche nation, who informs us that his nation is in an attitude of hostilities towards us.' Captain Carey noted, 'The savage Camancha Indians is near at hand. We expect soon to have a fight with them.'

The *Sydney Gazette* for 28 June 1836 published an article with the title *Interview with a Tribe of American Indians*, which gave an interesting review of the region and an idea of life in an Indian village in Texas at the time. It appeared in the section 'American Intelligence' and stated, 'By the *Celt*, by way of Liverpool, we have received a file of United States papers, the *New York Daily Advertiser*, to a recent date:

On the 19th July we again resumed our march, under the guidance of the Pawnee Mohawk, who, to my mind, proved himself to be a treacherous villain; for he led us a circuitous route for three days, over an excessively rugged rocky country, and amid inconveniencies of every description; on our return to the encampment, we traversed a beautiful

46

prairie and the distance did not exceed forty five miles. Yet for one I did not regret it, for our way led through scenery not exceeded, I hardly believe equalled. I have read of the Alps and have seen paintings of the most celebrated portion of the Alpine scenery. The Alps are higher, but in sublimity, grandeur and general effect, they must, and in time will yield the palm to the hitherto unknown, unvisited Pawnee Peaks. Here the gradual peaks, the beetling precipice, the castellated battlement, the solitary tower, the glittering vista, disclosing in its turn distant views of new grandeur; all the rich combinations of mountain scenery are thrown together, forming an unrivalled whole, which in years to come will be the goal to travellers on earth.

On the evening of the 21st, we reached the goal of our enterprise, the long sought Pawnee village. Here was a new matter of wonder. We approached a sweep of perpendicular mountains whose tops are wholly inaccessible to the human foot from this side, and reached the village through the passage which leads to it, a narrow defile which one hundred good men, with a proper armament, and a good engineer could keep against the countless legions, that Napoleon led to Moscow. Alter passing this defile, we immediately entered the village situated in a beautiful bottom on the margin of a river, supposed by some to be the main Red river, but which is only a principal fork in that stream. Like others of the southern rivers, its bottom is a flat bed of fine sand, that mountains nearly the same level all the way across, the water now but a few inches deep; yet unlike the water of the Kenhawa Saline.

When this stream is full, it is 500 yards wide and about ten feet deep. The natives say that the salt taste proceeds from beds of salt about 20 miles above, and exhibited in quantities that they had procured there. Our arrival here was timely; for we were hungry having nothing to eat. They had plenty of good corn just in good eating order; pumpkins, squashes, water and musketeers, together with dried buffalo meat. For supplies of these articles we gave them tobacco, tin cups, buttons, the yellow stripes of our pantaloons, &c. but when we offered them money they laughed at us, for these unsophisticated beings knew nothing of its value.

When we could explain to them the use of anything, they would trade for it but as we could not make them sensible of the use of money, none of it would they have. They called themselves Towea Indians and appear amiable and industrious. The women are real beauties; yes, real first rate light-copper beauties, for devil take the ugly one that I saw that was less than a 'centurion', which word a schoolmate of mine defined to be a person one hundred years old, and got flogged for his pains.

On the 22d and 23d, the Kiewa, Waco, and Comanche Indians arrived; and our little band was surrounded by between three and four thousand warriors; yet we trembled not. On the 14th the treaty proceeded, and by it among other things we recovered a little boy, the son of Gabriel Martin, a wealthy planter of Louisiana. He had gone up with some friends early last spring, on a hunting excursion, to the False Washita, and whilst separated from the rest, was attacked by the Indians and killed, and his son taken prisoner. They concealed the boy on our approach, and he probably would never have been liberated had it not been for a negro, likewise a prisoner, who informed us where he was concealed. He was 7 or 8 years old and unusually intelligent.

4

ENTER THE ARENA

The mission chapel at the south-west corner of the Alamo measured 75ft long, 62ft wide and 22ft high, with walls of solid masonry 4ft thick. Mexican army engineers had constructed some gun platforms by using materials from the roof of the chapel, and Colonel Neill charged Green B. Jameson, a lawyer turned engineer, to make some improvements.

A succession of outer buildings ringed the main plaza and parade ground, which created a perimeter wall about 12ft high. The fortified main gate and the hospital were at the south, the soldiers and artillery quarters known as the low barracks to the east, a timber and earth barricade formed the north wall, and the officers' barracks, headquarters and command posts created the west wall. Gun ramps mounted by cannon were placed at strategic points all around the defences and firing ramps were constructed simply by piling mounds of earth against the inner ramparts. The most vulnerable point was a gap of about fifty paces to the south-east at the front of the chapel. Jameson erected a wooden stake palisade to bridge the gap, supported by a ditch and an abattis of wooden stakes with their sharpened points facing outward.

The Mexicans had also left behind about twenty field pieces of various calibres and several hundred pounds of gunpowder. It was of poor quality and was no use when it came to firing muskets, so it was stored in the little side room at the north corner of the chapel ready to be ignited if and when the Mexicans assaulted the Alamo and all seemed lost.

Enrique Esparza stated that the walls were surrounded on the outside by a ditch "as deep as two men", and that a draw bridge spanning this moat afforded the means of ingress and egress to and from the place. It is known that such a wall and moat did exist and Esparza's familiarity with this is another proof of the genuineness of his story.

The Texans decided to send an expedition to attack and seize the Mexican port of Matamoros, with the intention of preventing the Centralists from returning to Texas. The expedition was led by Frank Johnson and James Grant, who convinced about 200 of the volunteers stationed at Bexar to accompany them. While preparations were under way, Johnston and Grant ordered the Bexar garrison to be stripped of most of its food, clothing and horses to outfit their expedition.

Consequently, both companies of the New Orleans Greys underwent a series of organisational changes. Captain Cook had mustered sixty-four men after the siege of Bexar, but all but twenty-two members of Breece's unit were dispersed into other companies. Those who remained were under the command of Captain Baugh, and when he became garrison adjutant William Blazeby was appointed captain and took command of the company. Captain Blazeby's company of New Orleans Greys, which is said to have numbered fifty-four, were among the initial detachment that entered the Alamo on 14 January 1836, and proudly hoisted their standard.

Captain Carey's artillerymen entered at about the same time. He wrote:

The force here is commanded by Lt-Colonel J C Neill, who has his quarters in the Town, which is called the left wing of the forces, and your brother William has the command of the Alamo, which is called the right wing. I am subject to the orders of Colonel Neill, but he thinks a great deal of my judgment and consults me about a number of the proceedings before he issues an order.

I cannot close without saying something about my *Invincibles*, as I call them, about twenty of my company (although the whole has been tried and I know them all) that will (to use their words) wade through hell when I am at their head if I should give the order. O, sister could you but see me at the head of those brave men marching forward (undismayed) to perform their duty. To relate circumstances of their bravery it would fill a large book. When the enemy, ten to one has marched up as if they in one minute would send us all to eternity to see the *invincible* rush forward and *charge* upon them and put them to flight except those we would either kill or take prisoners. We have had many such skirmishes since we left home.

A circumstance occurred the other day which I must relate. A man for disobedience of orders and bad conduct was ordered to be arrested (he was not under my command). The officer who received this order took a file of men and attempted to arrest him. He resisted and swore with pistols in his hands that he would shoot down the first man that attempted his arrest. The officer retreated without him. The colonel immediately sent an order to me informing me of the circumstances and requesting me to take a file of my *Invincibles* and bring the culprit to trial. I ordered three of the brave to prepare immediately. I buckled on my sword and went to him.

He was with two others, who also swore he would not be taken. I approached him with my men, and he told me if I came one step further he would certainly shoot me down, and the other two swore the same; and with great confidence too, as he had put the other off. But he soon found himself mistaken. My men wanted to rush immediately upon them, but I ordered them to halt, and I walked up to him, and with a mild tone told him to disarm himself or I would cut him asunder. He sheepishly laid down his pistols and gave himself up. However, the other two swore still that we would not take him.

I significantly looked up and told them if they attempted to move or put their finger on the trigger of their arms that they should fall on the spot they stood. I then walked up to them and took their arms likewise. My men stopped where I ordered them, watching minutely their movements, ready at the twinkling of an eye to do what I should say.

I told them to take those gentlemen to the guardhouse, which was done, and there they remained until trial. The court martial passed a sentence, or should have passed a sentence of death upon the first. I found it out and went into my room and wrote two notes; one to the court and the other to the colonel, and the sentence was remitted, and he was drummed out of the army. They all said that nothing but the *Invincibles* with Captain Carey could have taken them as he expected to die anyway if he was tried.

When anything of a dangerous character is to be done its by order Captain Carey will take a file from a company of his men and go immediately and – it's always done.

According to the account of Doctor John Sutherland, who had travelled to Gonzales at the request of Colonel Travis, and in the company of John William Smith (1792–1845), Captain William Patton and eleven men, including Sutherland himself, arrived at San Antonio on 18 January; although Doctor Sutherland and Captain Patton left as couriers before the final battle. With the unit was Doctor Sutherland's 17-year-old nephew, William DePriest Sutherland, a medical student at Le Grange College at Tuscumbia in Alabama.

Dr Sutherland recorded:

At this time the Texians had well nigh consumed everything they had on hand in the way of provisions. Grant and Johnson had left them but a small supply of coffee, sugar and salt which had long since disappeared, and none of these necessaries were to be found though they might have had ever so much money to buy them.

51

Their meat they obtained by driving the beef from the prairies just as they needed it, and as they never had more at one time than would serve them more than twenty-four hours, it so happened that they were in need just at that time. They were out of corn from which they made their bread and had no money to purchase more. Though Travis afterwards thought that the Lord was on his side upon the promise that, 'he would provide for the upright,' if he had claimed his favour under the circumstances it would have been upon the score that, 'He chasteneth whom he loveth.'

James Bowie and James Bonham entered the Alamo with about thirty men on 19 January. Bowie had been in command of about twenty Tejanos during the siege of Bexar and Doctor Sutherland stated that a few days after these reinforcements arrived: 'Some twenty Mexicans of the city joined them.'

Having learned of the desperate situation among the men, Houston had instructed Bowie to demolish the Alamo and remove the cannon. However, he had been allowed to use his own discretion on this and he was impressed by the work the men had put in. Bowie and Neill agreed that it was impossible to remove the twenty-four captured cannon without oxen, mules or horses. They did not want to abandon that much firepower, and having decided not to carry out the order Bowie wrote to the Governor on 2 February urging that the Alamo be held.

Among Bowie's men was Private Joseph M. Hawkins, who was born in Ireland in 1799. He left London on the *Philadelphia* and arrived in New York on 1 July 1833, travelling to Texas by way of Louisiana. He had served as an express rider to Sam Houston and he was a strong supporter of Governor Henry Smith, and an advocate of Texas independence.

Lieutenant Edward McCafferty was born in Ireland in about 1800. He is believed to have arrived in Texas in 1828, having received a land grant as a single man at San Patricio in South Texas from the Mexican government. He was described as 'a little Irishman', and a resident of Refugio County, near Matagorda Bay on the Gulf Coast, which had a large Irish population.

Robert McKinney was born at County Tyron in Ireland in 1809, his parents being named Samuel and Elizabeth. He left his widowed mother and siblings in 1835 bound for America, and disembarked from the ship *Delaware* in New Orleans. He took up temporary residence in Tennessee. His name is listed under the Irish flag at the Alamo memorial chapel. A land bounty of 640 acres was issued to his heirs on 7 January 1860.

Jackson J. Rusk was born in Ireland in 1810, and probably arrived in New Orleans, which was the largest harbour in the region, and was a resident of Nacogdoches. He registered for a land title in Lorenzo de Zavala's colony on 30 September 1835, but the transaction was never completed. He joined the military in 1835 and became a marksman in Captain William Baker's Company.

Governor Smith sent a unit of forty men of Texas Regular Cavalry to reinforce the garrison, led by Lieutenant Colonel William Barret 'Buck' Travis. Nine of them deserted on the way, and the remaining thirty-one arrived at the Alamo on 3 February. With them was a young Negro named Joe, who was Travis's slave. They included a mounted unit under Captain John Hubbard Forsyth, a 38-year-old widower, who had been raised on a farm in New York State. He was third in command at the Alamo. Lieutenant Cleveland Kinloch Simmons, a 20-year-old from South Carolina, would make a name for himself during the siege.

On 6 February, Davy Crockett and several other volunteers led by Captain William B Harrison rode to San Antonio de Bexar and camped just outside the town. They were later greeted by James Bowie and Antonio Menchaca, and taken to the nearby home of Erasmo Seguin. Crockett and his men finally entered the Alamo on 8 February. Known as the Tennessee Mounted Volunteers, five of them had travelled to Nacogdoches together, two of them being teenagers. It has never been certain how many men were with this unit or what their names were, but I believe Jesse Benton was with them.

Of Davy Crockett's arrival at the Alamo, Doctor Sutherland stated:

Colonel David Crockett arrived a few days later with twelve others, direct from Tennessee. Crockett was immediately offered a command by Travis, and called upon by the crowd for a speech. The former honour he would not accept, but mounted a goods box on the Civil Plaza, among prolonged cheers of the people. The applause, however, was followed by profound silence, when the full-toned voice of the distinguished speaker rose gradually above the audience and fell with smooth and lively accent upon the ears of all. Its sound was familiar to many who had heard it in days past, while the hearts of all beat a lively response to the patriotic sentiments which fell from his lips. Frequently applause greeted him, as he related in his own peculiar style some of those jolly anecdotes with which he often regaled his friends and which he, only, could tell with appropriate grace. He alluded frequently to his past career and during the course of his remarks stated that not long since he had been a candidate for Congress in his native State and that during the canvass he told his constituents that 'if they did not elect him, they might all go to – and he would go to Texas.' After which he concluded in substance as follows: 'And fellow citizens, I am among you. I have come to your country, though not, I hope, through any selfish motive whatever. I have come to aid you all that I can in your noble cause. I shall identify myself with your interests, and all the honor that I desire is that of defending as a high private, in common with my fellow-citizens, the liberties of our common country.' This made many a man who had not known him before Colonel Crockett's friend.

Of the situation at the Alamo, Doctor Sutherland stated: 'When reaching San Antonio we found the forces there in a manner of destitute ... Colonel James C. Neill, who was then in command, readily foresaw that something must be done, and, that too without delay, or his position would be abandoned and left subject to recapture by the enemy should they return. He therefore determined to procure, if possible, a portion of a donation of five thousand dollars which had been given to the cause of Texas by Harry Hill of Nashville, Tennessee, and accordingly he left Bexar about the twelfth or fifteenth of February for that purpose.' [It was actually 14 February.]

In his absence Bowie and Travis assumed joint command, with Bowie commanding the volunteers and Travis the regulars.

On 20 February a Mexican sympathetic to the Texan cause came in and reported that Santa Anna's troops had crossed the Rio Grande about two days earlier – only 120 miles from San Antonio. However, several such false rumours had been circulated and the garrison did not take the warning too seriously.

On 22 February the people of San Antonio and most of the Alamo garrison attended a fiesta to commemorate George Washington's birthday, during which there was lively dancing, good food and the alcohol flowed freely. A Mexican spy, said to have been Santa Anna himself, apparently attended the festivities in disguise to gather intelligence and warn the Tejanos to get out of town. People drifted home after the party to sleep off the effects of their revelling, and by midnight the town fell quiet. However, as daylight appeared a steady stream of carts and wagons carrying people and their possessions began to leave town. Travis became both concerned and suspicious, but it took him several hours to confirm that elements of the Mexican army were approaching. The San Fernando Church bell rang, and on rushing to the tower with Doctor Sutherland the lookout pointed to specks of flashing light flickering in the distance.

Doctor Sutherland and John Smith rode out to see what was causing the flashes, and came upon Mexican cavalry of the Delores Regiment preparing to advance on the town. On their hasty return they discovered that Travis had moved his headquarters and the entire force to the Alamo, and, having realised that he may be in for a siege, he ordered that a herd of cattle should be driven into the Alamo compound, and his men confiscated several sacks of corn that the Tejanos had left behind.

***

The Mina Mounted Rangers (Bastrop) had seven men in the Alamo, one of them being James E. Stewart, who was born in England. Findmypast parish baptisms record only one man who matches his name. James Edward Stewart was born to Daniel and Mary Stewart, on 22 January 1807, and he was baptised at St Mary's Church in Hanover Square, Westminster, London, on 1 February 1807. He arrived in Texas in 1836.

John James Tumlinson raised a unit of Texas Rangers in Mina, and they were known as the Mina Mounted Rangers. They left the town to go to join up with the Gonzales Rangers. One unit headed for Cibolo Creek to the east of San Antonio to meet the Gonzales men, while the other rode towards the Alamo. Major Robert McAlpine met with both the Ranger units on 28 February 1836.

Captain Philip Dimmitt, a Texas trader and merchant, had arrived at Bexar with about thirty volunteers on 24 January, and was appointed storekeeper, his warehouse at Dimmitt's Landing serving as a depot for government stores landed at Lavaca Bay. Though many of his volunteers returned home on 3 February, Dimmitt remained in San Antonio scouting for Travis and Bowie until the first full day of the siege on 24 February.

David L. Wilson remained at the Alamo after Captain Dimmitt left. He was born in Scotland in 1807, the son of James Wilson and his wife, Susanna (formerly Wesley) and lived in Nacogdoches with his wife, Ophelia.

Two other Brits who are known to have entered the Alamo were Richard W. Ballentine and George Brown. Ballentine was born in Scotland in 1814. In 1820, aged 6, he travelled to America with his family aboard the *Criterion* bound for New York. He lived in Alabama before boarding the *Santiago* and disembarked on 9 December 1835, bound for Galveston. He and the other passengers signed a statement declaring: 'We have left every endearment at our respective places of abode in the United States of America, to maintain and defend our brethren, at the peril of our lives, liberties and fortunes.' He enlisted in the Texas army as a rifleman.

George Brown was born in England in 1801 and lived at Yazoo in Mississippi before settling in Gonzales. He was one of four men named George Brown in the Texas army during the Texas Revolution. There was a Robert Brown on the Gray list stated to have been with Travis's Company.

5

TRIUMVIRATE

James Bowie was born at Logan County in Kentucky on 10 April 1796. Stories of his frontier adventures had made him a folk hero and he had become a prominent landowner. According to Dublin-born Nicholas Doran Proby Maillard (1810–80) in his 1842 book *The History of the Republic of Texas*: 'Bowie was a reckless drunkard, who had squandered his property, and was subsequently obliged to fly from his country (the United States), for slaying a man in a duel. This fact is well known in Texas, and was thus told me by a friend of Bowie's, who was present when Rezin Bowie fought a duel with knives across a table at the Alamo, a few days before Santa Anna took it.' [Resin was his brother.]

Several newspapers around the British Empire recorded that:

James Bowie's first duel was fought at Natchez on the Mississippi River, in the autumn of 1834. A serious dispute arose at a card table, in the middle of the day, between Bowie and a man named Black. The lie was given by Bowie to his opponent, and at the same moment drawing his knife (which was a case one, with a blade about four inches long, such as the Americans always carry in their pockets), he challenged the man to fight, which was accepted; and Black having taken his seat opposite Bowie, at a small square table, the conflict began. It lasted about twenty minutes, during which time both parties were severely cut, when Bowie rose from the table, and with a desperate oath rushed upon his antagonist, who immediately fell dead at his feet.

The inconvenience felt by Bowie on this occasion, from the smallness of the knife, having called forth the exercise of his debauched and sanguinary mind, he invented a weapon which would enable him, to use his own words, 'to rip a man up right away.' This task he accomplished during his exile in Texas, and which was the only legacy he could leave his young and adopted republic; indeed, it is all she can show of her citizen, his body having been burnt by the Mexicans, and his ashes swept from the face of the earth by the passing winds.

There have been several versions concerning the history of the Bowie knife, but it is believed that it first came to public attention during the Sandbar Fight on an island in the middle of the Mississippi River near present-day Vidalia in Louisiana, on 19 September 1827. The middle of the Mississippi River marked the border between Louisiana to the west and Mississippi to the east. Samuel L. Wells III and Doctor Thomas H. Maddox had agreed to fight a duel to settle a number of grievances between them. James Bowie was present as a supporter of Sam Wells. During the desperate struggle, in which Bowie was wounded several times, he used the knife for the first time and thus the legend was born.

A contemporary account and anecdotes appeared in numerous newspapers in the English-speaking world on 13 September 1890, which stated:

James Bowie, whose patronymic designates the most murderous weapon ever handled by Christian men, was by no means the truculent desperado one would have imagined him to have been from the connection of his name with the knife that has gained such evil notoriety. Although, like most Americans of his time and surroundings, he was a law unto himself, there was a strain of rough and ready justice and chivalry in his pugnacity which removes his name from the category of vulgar ruffians, and his death was pathetic and honourable.

His family first settled in Maryland, of which State one Robert Bowie was elected Governor in 1803. His parents having migrated to the South, James was born in Burke County, Georgia, about 1790. The family finally settled down in Catahoula Parish, Louisiana, in 1802.

The celebrated faction fight, which brought the Bowie knife into prominence, occurred in August, 1827. In that year, there was considerable rivalry in speculations connected with the rich, virgin cotton lands in Mississippi and Louisiana. This led to bad blood and frequent encounters between the speculators, among whom were to be found almost every man of wealth and good social position in the large and rich Parish of Rapides.

Doctor Maddox, Major [Norris] Wright, and the Blanchards [Alfred and Carey] were principals of one faction; the Cunys [Doctor Richard and General Samuel], Wellses [Samuel and Jefferson], and Bowie of the other. A duel, between Maddox and Samuel Wells was arranged to be fought on a sand bar, opposite Natchez, in Mississippi, outside the State limits. Colonel [Robert A.] Crane, second to Maddox, had a long-standing feud with General Cuny and James Bowie.

The duellists exchanged two shots without effect, and their difficulty was amicably adjusted. Then appeared on the scene General Wells and Cuny, armed with pistols, and James Bowie carrying a huge knife in addition to his pistol. On seeing them, the partisans of Maddox and Crane crossed over from the Louisiana side to join in the affray which appeared inevitable.

Cuny, drawing his pistol, advanced to Crane, remarking pleasantly that it was a good time to settle their difficulty, but was restrained by his brother. Bowie and Crane fired at each other. Bowie was hit; but, drawing his knife, went for Crane, who was watching Cuny, now released from his brother's grasp. Crane fired, and mortally wounded Cuny. Then, clubbing his pistol and adroitly evading a thrust from the formidable knife, he felled Bowie to the ground. Crane retreated towards his advancing friends one of whom, Wright, attacked Bowie with a sword-stick, wounding him. The latter, who was the more powerful of the two, closed with Wright, and, dragging him to the ground plunged his knife into the heart of his opponent. By this time the fight had become general, ending in the death of six and the wounding of fifteen of the participants.

The knife thus fatally used for the first time by James Bowie was fashioned out of a blacksmith's rasp by Resin Pleasant Bowie, his elder brother, who made a suitable little speech on handing the fraternal gift to James. 'The knife,' said he, 'is of a strong and admirable temper. It is more trustworthy in the hands of a strong man than a pistol, for it will not snap. Crane and Wright are both your enemies. They are from Maryland, the birthplace of our ancestors, and are as brave as you are, but not so cool. They are both inferior in strength to yourself, and therefore not your equal in a close fight. They are both dangerous, but Wright the most so. Keep this knife always with you. It will be your friend in a last resort, and may save your life.' After this baptism of blood the knife was taken by Resin Bowie to Philadelphia, where a cutler manufactured wholesale from the original model.

Two anecdotes, of the many recorded, will serve as illustrations of the rough justice and natural chivalry of character that distinguished James Bowie:

In 1833 a young Southerner, returning to Natchez with his newly-married wife and a large sum of money, was marked down for plunder by one of the many gangs of card-sharpers that used to infest the Mississippi steamboats in former days. In due course the victim was thoroughly fleeced, but before this came about the boat was boarded above Vicksburg by a tall, erect, and dignified personage, very much like a preacher in appearance.

Maddened by his losses and drink, the young man tried to jump overboard, but was seized in time by the new passenger, and handed over to the care of his wife in their cabin to await developments.

Returning to the gamblers, the clerical-looking gentleman excited their predatory instincts by the exhibition of a well-filled wallet. Play was resumed, and at daybreak the stakes amounted to £20,000, of which a third had been contributed by the stranger. The dealer, at the last, slipped a card to a confederate, whose wrist was instantly grasped as in a vice, while a murderous-looking knife compelled him to lay his cards on the table. Instead of five there were six cards. In the uproar which ensued the stranger, when asked his name, quietly replied 'James Bowie'. Two of the gang suddenly collapsed, for they had heard of him before, but the third, who had not, persisted in having satisfaction then and there with pistols.

Promptly accepting the challenge, Bowie took the precaution to sweep all the money on the board into his hat, which he carried off and delivered to the victim's wife. Mounting again to the hurricane deck he took his appointed place, 12 yards from his opponent. At the word both fired. The gambler fell, and after a convulsive struggle rolled off the deck into the river. Bowie re-pocketed one-third of the money, which was his own, and returned the remainder, amounting to within a few dollars of his losses, to the young man from Natchez; and, not desiring to be made a hero of, left the boat for Rodney.

A Methodist minister, who related the incident himself, journeying from Louisiana to Texas, was overtaken on the road by a horseman armed with rifle, pistols, and knife. They jogged along together pleasantly for several days, neither thinking of asking the other his name.

Arriving at a Texan town, which had become the headquarters of desperadoes and fugitives from justice in every State, the minister notified his intention of preaching that night in the Court House, which was duly filled with a congregation mainly composed of men. All joined in the hymn, and sang it well, but the opening of the sermon was saluted with braying, hooting, and other discordant sounds. Every successive attempt was met with similar interruptions. When the minister's travelling companion, who, unknown to him, was present, suddenly rose and said: 'Men, this man has come here to preach to you. You need preaching to, and I'll be blanked if he shan't preach to you. The next man that disturbs him shall fight me. My name's Jim Bowie.' After this announcement, no preacher ever had a more respectful and attentive congregation.

Bowie became a naturalised Mexican, and he married Maria Ursula Fructuosa Veramendi in San Antonio on 25 April 1831. She was the daughter of Governor Juan Martin del Carmen Veramendi, and his wife, Maria Josepha Candida Gertrudus (formerly Navarro). They had a daughter named Marie Elve (born 20 March 1832 at Monclova, Coahuila de Tejas); and James Veramendi (born at Monclova, Coahuila de Tejas, on 18 July 1833). However, a cholera epidemic hit the town of Monclova and Bowie's wife and children contracted it. A doctor named Ignacio Sendejas attempted to cure the disease with a concoction made from peyote, a species of cactus, but the experiment failed and they all died on 10 September 1833. All three are buried in San Fernando Cathedral; as are Governor Veramendi and his wife, who died of cholera in Monclova on 26 September 1833.

In his despair at such a tragic loss, he began drinking heavily, and his habits were weakening his constitution and damaging his health.

***

David Crockett was born at Limestone in Greene County, Tennessee, on 17 August 1786. According to his autobiography, his father was John Crockett, who he believed was of Irish descent, and who became a farmer in Pennsylvania. His mother was named Rebecca (formerly Hawkins), who was born in Maryland. Davy was the fifth son of six in the family of nine children.

The early years of his life were spent in the backwoods of eastern Tennessee, where he became well known for his extraordinary ability at hunting and his masterful storytelling. From 1813 to 1815 he served as a scout in frontier militia units during the Creek War.

William Kennedy wrote:

The American frontiersman may be said to exist in a state of continual warfare. He experiences the toils of active service in clearing and cultivating his ground, its anxieties in guarding against a treacherous enemy, and its perils in encountering that enemy, and the beast of prey. Confident in what he dare do and can endure, with all the feelings of his nature roused to vengeance by some sanguinary Indian outrage, he sallies forth in pursuit of the exulting savage. Following on his trail, he traverses the prairies, swimming the streams, noting every impression on grass, sand, twig, and tuft, reckless of fatigue, hunger, and cold, until he overtakes the remorseless foe, whom at great numerical disadvantage, he is almost certain to defeat. To men of this class, a campaign is a party of pleasure, and they require only the exercise and discipline of the regular soldier to make the best soldiers in the world. Mounted on a favourite horse, armed with a trusty rifle, and accompanied by their dogs, they can explore their way through the woods by the sun and the bark of the trees. Clad in their usual homely dress, an otter skin cunningly folded and sowed is the depository of tobacco, ammunition, and the moans for kindling a fire; a wallet slung behind the saddle contains sustenance for man and horse. On the march, a small daily allowance of maize suffices the latter, which, at the evening encampment, is stripped of his furniture and hobbled (two of his legs fastened together), and thus left to indulge his appetite on the abundant herbage. It is of such materials that the militia of Texas and the south- western states of the Union is composed.

Crockett became involved in local politics from about 1817, starting out as justice of the peace for Lawrence County in Tennessee. In 1818, he was elected to the positions of lieutenant colonel of his local militia regiment and town commissioner of Lawrenceburg. He resigned those positions in 1821 to campaign for a seat in the state legislature, which he won by a landslide. He was elected to the Tennessee legislature again in 1823. Then, in 1825, he ran for Congress. He was defeated by the incumbent, Adam Alexander. However, when he ran again in 1827, he won easily. He was re-elected in 1829, but experienced ever increasing friction between himself and President Andrew Jackson. As a result, he was defeated in the election of 1831. He regained his seat by a narrow margin in 1833, but lost for good in 1835.

With wounded pride and empty purse, he made a final speech to his constituents: 'I told [my constituents], moreover, of my services, pretty straight up and down ... and I also told them of the manner in which I had been knocked down and dragged out, and that I did not consider it a fair fight anyhow they could fix it. I put the ingredients in the cup pretty strong I tell you, and I concluded my speech by telling them that I was done with politics for the present, and that they might all go to hell, and I would go to Texas.'

Several British Empire newspapers recorded the following anecdote:

David Crockett, while at Washington-on-the-Brazos, visiting a menagerie which opened there for exhibition, and stopping before the cage of a huge baboon, exclaimed, after gazing a while upon the grotesque quadrumana:

'Bless me! That fellow looks exactly like Tom **** of Alabama,' naming an honourable member of Congress from that State, then on duty in Washington.

'Sir!' sounded an indignant voice at his elbow.

Davy turned and beheld, with a lady upon either arm, the very member whom he had likened to the baboon.

'Really, sir,' said Crockett. 'I had no idea that you were so near. Had I known it, I shouldn't have spoken as I did.'

The honourable member was irate, and in language slightly tinctured with threatening, demanded an apology.

'Oh, certainly,' replied David, good-naturedly. 'I am ready to apologise. Yes, yes – but' – and he looked from the honourable member to the animal in the cage, and from the animal back to the honourable member, who, by the way, had never been deemed a handsome man – 'really, I don't know which I ought to apologise to – you or the baboon!'

General de Cos remembered Crockett as a 'good-looking and well-dressed man', and Enrique Esparza stated, 'I remember Crockett. He was a tall, slim man, with black whiskers.'

Davy Crockett and his nephew William Patton got into Nacogdoches in 5 January 1836. All the men named formed a small unit of sixty-five troopers known as the Tennessee Volunteer Force. On 14 January 1836, the commanding officer, Captain William B Harrison, arrived at the offices of Irish-born Colonel John Forbes, a lawyer, and the first judge of the municipality, to take the Oath of Allegiance. Harrison and Forbes had both come to the town from Ohio. The colonel immediately wrote out the following form:

> I do solemnly swear that I will bear true allegiance to the provisional government of Texas, or any future government that hereafter may be declared, and that I will serve her honestly and faithfully against all her enemies and opposers whatsoever, and observe and obey the orders of the Governor of Texas, the orders and decrees of the present and future authorities and the orders of the officers appointed over me according to the rules and articles for the government of Texas so help me God.

Upon offering it to Crockett he refused to sign it, saying that he was willing to take an oath to support any future republican, but could not subscribe his name to this form, as the future government might be despotic; the colonel therefore inserted the word republican between the words future and government, and Crockett signed it. His nephew signed it three names down from his.

Evidence suggests that parties of volunteers signed the Allegiance on separate days and Colonel Forbes gave the date of the statement as 14 January so not to confuse matters.

***

Although he was a descendant of the wealthy family of Travers of Preston in Lancashire, William Barret 'Buck' Travis was the least-known in Britain of the main men who fought at the Alamo; and, unlike Santa Anna, Bowie and Crockett, little information can be found about him in British newspapers prior to the battle.

He was a 26-year-old lawyer, the oldest of at least eleven children from South Carolina. He was a married man, and had recently served as a scout in the Texan cavalry around San Antonio.

In a series of articles connected with the Great War entitled 'Soldier Families', the *London Observer* of 28 February 1915, stated:

May I reply to Special Constable's letter, and say that of the soldier families the Travers family have beaten the record. For instance, Sir Robert Travers, Rifle Brigade, was one of six brothers, four in the Rifle Brigade and two in the Navy. These six brothers married, had between them 24 sons, and put them into the Army. At the same time that Sir Robert and his three brothers were in the Rifle Brigade, two first cousins were in also, making six Traverses in the regiment at the same time. It is a known fact that no other family has produced so many soldiers, and they are nicknamed the 'Fighting Traverses'. They have the cockleshell, and fought at the Crusades; their name is carved at Battle Abbey, and is on the Battle Abbey roll.

They have a clear and authentic descent from Baron Robert de Travers, who in 1067 married the heiress of Nateby in Lancashire, and obtained Nateby and Tulketh Hall and Mount Travers in that county. Several members of the family who were serving in the regular army before the war are at the front, and Captain H . Travers is among the killed.

Admiral Sir Eaton Travers was over 100 times engaged with the enemy, and eight times mentioned for gallant conduct. Mr Travers, of Metung, belongs to a branch of the family. He has 14 nephews at the front at the present time.

According to the family Bible, William was born on 9 August 1809, although the date was more likely 1 August. His great-grandfather was born in North Carolina, but he is known to have returned to Britain to receive his medical education.

William was the eldest of eleven children to Mark Travis and his wife Jemima Elizabeth (formerly Stalworth, 1790–1867). At the time of his birth the family home was at Mine Creek near the Red Bank community (now Saluda) in Edgefield County in South Carolina.

***

Four defenders are named separately on the San Antonio cenotaph, the other being James Butler Bonham. He was born on 20 February 1807, at Red Banks (now Saluda) in Edgefield County, South Carolina. He was a son of Captain James Butler Bonham (1766–1815), of Maryland, and his wife, Sophia Butler Smith (1780–1858); and is believed to have been a second cousin of William Travis.

He was educated at South Carolina College from 1823, being expelled in 1827, and gave up his law practice in Pendleton in October 1835. He then organised a unit of volunteers in Alabama named the Mobile Grays, with which he reached Texas in the following month. He began practising law at Brazoria. On 1 December he wrote to Sam Houston from San Felipe, volunteering his services for the Texas cause, and he was commissioned as a 2nd lieutenant in the Texas cavalry on 20 December 1835. He and Houston developed a good relationship, and Houston recommended that he be promoted major. He seems to have acted independently of any unit after that. His boyhood home (Flat Grove) is the only house of an Alamo defender known to exist today.

6

EJERCITO DE OPERACIÓNES

The *New York Commercial Advertiser* for 13 May 1835 reported:

A letter from a personal friend of President Santa Anna to a gentleman in this city, dated April 15th, gives some further particulars of the contemplated revolution. The original motive seems to have been founded in Nullification doctrines – or something very like them.

General Santa Anna set out for the army on the 18th, his forces amounting to five thousand excellent troops. General Alvarez with one thousand men, was at the gates of Acapulco on the first, and no doubt was entertained of his making himself master of that town. A small division had been despatched by Santa Anna in pursuit of him.

Symptoms of disaffection had appeared at Valladolid and Puebla, and it was expected that on any reverse of fortune, the states of Tamaulipas, San Luis and Coahuila would take an active part against Santa Anna. The clergy and land proprietors had given him 300,000 dollars wherewith to carry on the war, the Treasury being completely exhausted.

The Texans had underestimated Santa Anna, who considered the Texas Revolution to be a personal affront and had decided on a swift winter campaign to surprise them. He presented himself in the district of Tacubaya in Mexico City on 28 November 1835, and arrived at San Luis Potosí in December 1835 to organise an 'Ejercito de Operaciónes' – 'Army of Operations', consisting of about 3,000 men and twenty-one field pieces.

When he heard the news that the Mexican forces under General Cos had been defeated at San Antonio and had been forced out of Texas, the Generalissimo made an appeal in the city for finances and manpower and was successful in both. More than three thousand conscripts were yanked 'out of the fields', including prisoners and convicts. When he had got together enough men he marched northwards to Saltillo, the capital city of Coahuila y Tejas, where his army arrived on Thursday, 7 January. There he arranged his force into brigades. The Vanguard Brigade, led by Brigadier General Joaquín Ramírez y Sesma, consisted of about 1,400 men and eight guns; and a cavalry brigade of nearly three hundred troopers led by Colonel Juan José Andrade; Santa Anna was to accompany this brigade, with Colonel Almonte with him as his special advisor.

The First Brigade, led by Colonel Antonio Gaona, consisted of about the same number of men as the Vanguard, with six guns. Parts of this unit did not arrive at San Antonio until 8 March. The Second Brigade, commanded by Colonel Eugenio Tolosa, consisted of 1,700 men with six cannon. The Generalissimo sent General Jose de Urrea with 450 men eastwards to Matamoros, to deal with the Goliad rebels.

Each battalion comprised of one company of *cazadores* (a light infantry rifle company similar to French *chasseurs*), usually used as skirmishers; one company of *granaderos* (grenadier company), elite troops of the battalion usually used as reserves; and six companies of *fusilieros* (fusilier or line company). The infantry were armed with various types of British-made rifles, either Baker rifles, British light infantry muskets or East India-pattern muskets.

The trek northwards to Tejas, mostly at double pace, was a nightmare for most of the way. While under a burning hot sun and suffering the effects of dry dust that parched their throats, they began to suffer from lack of water and forage for the animals. Snow fell on northern Mexico. With only blankets and their uniform tunics for protection many *soldados* succumbed to the worsening conditions. General Urrea's division, advancing north from Matamoros, also encountered freezing weather. As they approached the Rio Grande on 13 February the temperature dropped from 62 to 46 degrees and a severe storm known as a 'Blue Norther', named from the blue-tinted edge of the weather disturbance, hit and they went from blistering heat to a chilling cold. This type of weather front is caused when a cold front sweeps down from the far north, gaining momentum as it travels. When the cold air meets with the warm, moist air of the Gulf of Mexico, it usually results in heavy snowfalls.

The Mexican Army crossed the Rio Grande into Tejas at the Paso de Francia, known as the San Antonio Crossing, on 16 February 1836, and, according to Colonel de la Pena, Santa Anna addressed his soldiers:

> Comrades in arms, our most sacred duties have brought us to these uninhabited lands and demand our engaging in combat against a rabble of wretched adventurers to whom our authorities have unwisely

given benefits that even Mexicans did not enjoy, and who have taken possession of this vast and fertile area, convinced that our own unfortunate internal divisions had rendered us incapable of defending our soil. Wretches! Soon will they become aware of their folly! Soldiers, our comrades have been shamefully sacrificed at Anahuac, Goliad and Bejar, and you are those destined to punish these murderers. My friends, we will march as long as the interests of the nation that we serve demand. The claimants to the acres of Texas land will soon know to their sorrow that their reinforcements from New Orleans, Mobile, Boston and New York, and other points north, whence they should never have come, are insignificant, and that Mexicans, generous by nature, will not leave unpunished affronts resulting in injury or discredit to their country, regardless of who the aggressor may be.

Some aspects of his speech mirrored the cause of why Britain had to send a Task Force to repatriate the Falklands Islands in 1982.

The force consisted of 452 men of the San Luis Potosi *Activo* Battalion, under Colonel Juan Morales; and 272 men of the Matamoros *Permanente* Battalion, under Colonel Jose Maria Romero. The battalion was named after Lieutenant General Fray Mariano Matamoros (1770–1814). There were also 274 men of the Jimenez *Permanente* Battalion, led by Colonel Jose Mariano Salas. The battalion was named after Lieutenant Colonel Jose Mariano Jimenez (1781–1811). In addition there were three hundred men of the Allende *Permanente* Battalion (Reserves). The battalion was named after Ignacio Jose de Allende (1769–1811). Finally, there were one hundred artillerymen with eight guns under Lieutenant Colonel Pedro y Ampudia Grimarest.

Moving among the Mexican troops and seemingly asking a lot of questions without being suspected of his true motives, was a fellow Mexican. He was Blas Maria Herrera (1802–78), who had been sent by his cousin Colonel Juan Sequin (1806–90) from Bexar, with whose unit he had fought at the siege of Bexar, to perform the dangerous task of collecting as much intelligence about Santa Anna's plans and the strength of the Mexican force as he could and report back to the Bexar garrison. He reported back to Colonel Seguin on the evening of 20 February, and Doctor Sutherland recorded:

About nine o'clock that night a council of war was held in Colonel Travis' room. Herrera was brought before it and required to report what he had seen. He reported that he had seen the army crossing the river and through enquiry had ascertained that the main body of the force, numbering thirty-five hundred, would travel slowly, but that the cavalry, fifteen hundred strong, would make a forced march for the purpose of taking the Texians by surprise. This created some considerable discussion. Some held that it was more authentic than anything that had reached them before, whilst a majority declared that it was only the report of a Mexican, and entitled to no more consideration than many others of a like character that were daily harangued throughout the country. The council adjourned without coming to any conclusion as to whether it was necessary to give any heeding to the warning or not.

On the same day, Jesse Benton, a good friend of Davy Crockett, wrote to a friend near Nacogdoches:

Official information has just reached us that Santa Anna has crossed the Rio Grande and is marching against us with a large army for the purpose of exterminating us. Nearly all our troops are riflemen; no body of infantry to lodge or to form squares or rush with and crush the enemy. We will die hard, for it will be truly victory or death with us. Our volunteers have consumed our provisions and a great many have left us – just what I expected. General Cos and his troops we are informed have broken their parole and are returning against us ... if we cannot defend the country in any other way, we can do it effectively by adopting the Russian mode of defense against Napoleon in 1812.

***

In a letter to his Minister of War, José Maria Tornel y Mendivil (1795–1853), Santa Anna wrote: 'On the twenty-third of this month at three o'clock in the afternoon I occupied [Bexar] ... My object had been to surprise [the Alamo garrison] at dawn the day before, but a hard rain prevented me from doing so.'

On the afternoon of Tuesday, 23 February, the first Mexican mounted troops of the Dolores Cavalry rode into San Antonio without opposition. Francisco Antonio Ruiz was the alcalde of the city and he recorded:

On the 23rd of February, 1836, at 2 p.m., General Santa Anna entered the city of San Antonio with a part of his army. This he effected without any resistances, the forces under the command of Travis, Bowie and Crockett having on the same day, at 8 a.m. learned that the Mexican army was on the banks of the Medina River, and concentrated in the Alamo.

In the evening they commenced to exchange fire with guns and from the 23rd of February to the 6th of March (in which the storming was made by Santa Anna), the roar of artillery and volleys of musketry were constantly heard.

An Irish artilleryman named Bill Ward, who had come to Bexar from New Orleans, had gained a reputation around the town for being drunk most of the time; although he had been given the rank of sergeant. However, as the garrison was making its way into the Alamo and the Mexican cavalry appeared, he was seen manning the artillery position at the Alamo main gate, calm and sober.

Dr Sutherland remembered, 'While they were retiring from the city to the Alamo they met twenty or thirty beeves [cattle] coming down Alamo Street (now Commerce Street), and gathered around them and drove them into the Alamo. They also got their bread by chance. During the hurry and excitement of the day a number of Mexican 'jacales' [shacks or huts] near the Alamo had been vacated. In them they found some eighty or ninety bushels of corn. These were their supplies during the siege.'

After the conflict Colonel de la Pena stated:

> The responsibility for the victims sacrificed at the Alamo, however, must rest on General Ramirez y Sesma rather than on the commander-in-chief. He knew that the enemy was at Bejar in small numbers and in the greatest destitution. When Sesma first sighted the town, the enemy was still engaged in the pleasures of a dance given the night before; he therefore could have, and should have prevented their taking refuge in the Alamo. Several came to inform him, indicating to him the points through which he might enter and the orders he should give and urging him earnestly, but he turned down these recommendations and the repeated requests, conducting himself with extraordinary uncertainty and weakness. We have seen how dearly his indecision was paid for. At the very moment when General Ramirez y Sesma was advised to enter Bejar, there were only ten men in the Alamo, and it would have required an equal number to take it. Had he just placed himself at the bridge over the San Antonio that connects the fort to the city, as he was advised, he would have prevented the enemy from taking refuge there, thus avoiding the painful catastrophe that I have just described.

As the Mexican army secured the town, Colonel Bowie sent his friend, Ensign Green Berry Jameson, who Bowie referred to as 'Benito', with a note for the Mexicans, which stated:

> Because a shot was fired from a cannon of this fort at the time a red flag was raised over the tower, and because a little afterwards they told me that a part of your army had sounded a parley, which was not heard before the firing of the shot, I wish, Sir, to ascertain if it be true that a parley was called, for which reason I send my second aid, Benito Jameson,

under guarantee of a white flag which I believe will be respected by you and your forces. God and Texas.

Jameson admitted the bad state they were in at the garrison, and expressed a wish that some honourable conditions should be proposed for surrender. The response was negative.

Later, a small unit of Mexican soldiers carrying a white flag was seen approaching the fort, and Travis sent Captain Robert C. Morris and Captain Albert Martin as emissaries to meet Santa Anna's adjutant, Colonel Juan Almonte, who demanded an unconditional surrender and rejected Martin's invitation to come to the Alamo and speak directly to Travis. His response, carried by Colonel Jose Batres, the adjutant major of the President General Santa Anna, was: 'I reply to you, according to the order of his Excellency, that the Mexican army cannot come to terms under any conditions with rebellious foreigners to whom there is no recourse left, if they wish to save their lives, than to place themselves immediately at the disposal of the Supreme Government from whom alone they may expect clemency after some considerations.'

On Captain Morris reporting this, Travis responded by firing a defiant cannon shot into the midst of the Mexican troops, which had halted on the main plaza, at the entrance of Commerce Street. To this Santa Anna responded by having a blood red flag displayed from the tower of San Fernando church, which indicated that the defenders would be given no mercy.

In his 'Victory or Death' letter, Colonel Travis stated: '... on 23 February the enemy in large force entered the city of Bexar, which could not be prevented, as I had not sufficient force to occupy both positions. Colonel Batres demanded surrender at discretion, calling us foreign rebels. I answered them with a cannon shot, upon which the enemy commenced a bombardment with a five inch howitzer, which together with a heavy cannonade, has kept up incessantly ever since. I instantly sent express to Colonel Fannin at Goliad, and the people of Gonzales and San Felipe.'

Colonel Almonte described in his diary how he saw the events of 23 February:

At 7:30am the army was put in march to the Potranca, one and a half Leagues – to the Creek of Leon or Del Medio, three and a half Leagues; and to Bexar, three Leagues; eight Leagues in all. [Note: One League is 3 miles.]

At half-league from Bexar the division halted on the hills of Alazan at 12:30 o'clock.

General Sesma arrived at 7:00am and did not advance to reconnoitre because he expected an advance of the enemy, which was about to be made according to accounts given by a spy of the enemy who was caught. There was water, though little, in a stream of Las Lomas del Alazan.

At 2:00 pm the army took up their march, the President and his staff in the van. The enemy, as soon as the march of the division was seen, hoisted the tri-coloured flag with two stars, designed to represent Coahuila and Texas. The President with all his staff advanced to Campo Santo (burying ground). The enemy lowered the flag and fled, and possession was taken of Bexar without firing a shot.

At 3:00 pm the enemy filed off to the fort of Alamo, where there was pieces of artillery; among them one 18-pounder: It appeared they had 130 men; during the afternoon four grenades were fired at them. The firing was suspended in order to receive a messenger, who brought a dispatch the contents of which appears in Number 1, and the answer which was given will be found in Number 2. I conversed with the bearer who was Jameson (G.B.) [Green Berry] and he informed me of the bad state they were in at the Alamo, and manifested a wish that some honourable conditions should be proposed for surrender. Another messenger afterwards came, (Martin) late a clerk in a house in New Orleans. He stated to me what Mr Travis said, 'that if I wished to speak with him, he would receive me with much pleasure.' I answered that it did not become the Mexican Government to make any propositions through me, and that I had only permission to hear such as might be made on the part of the rebels.

Sergeant Manuel Loranca of the Mexican army recalled in 1878: 'About nine in the morning [23 February], President Santa Anna arrived and joined with his escort and staff, the column which was now in the vicinity of San Antonio. We marched upon the place and were received by the fort with one or two cannon shots; those in the Alamo raising a red flag.'

***

It has always been accepted that the first meetings between the Mexicans and the defenders took place on the bridge at Alamo Street, which is now East Commerce Street. However, the author's research suggests that the meeting actually took place on the bridge that is now situated on East Crockett Street.

Doctor John Sutherland, an eyewitness, stated: 'After the entrance of the cavalry into the city which was affected without resistance, some few minutes passed when a white flag was seen descending Commerce Street. Major Morris and Captain Martin were commissioned to meet it and confer with its bearers. This meeting took place on a small foot

71

bridge which led from the Alamo to the city, crossing the river just above the one which now crosses on Commerce Street.'

The map prepared by Santa Anna's Commander of Engineers, Ignacio de Labastida, clearly shows just one footbridge over the San Antonio River, which is situated about where the bridge on East Crockett Street is today, and not as far around the bend in the river where East Commerce Street is situated. The same applies to the José Sánchez-Navarro plan. As stated by Doctor Sutherland: 'This meeting took place on a small foot bridge which led from the Alamo to the city, crossing the river just above the one which now crosses on Commerce Street.' The Labastida map shows no bridge of note on Commerce Street, and it is more likely to have been a small construction over a ditch. There were several ditches in the area, and James Bowie stated on 2 February 1836, that he 'would rather die in these ditches than give it up to the enemy'. It is also reasonable to suggest that after retreating into the Alamo for comparative safety, and knowing Santa Anna's ruthless reputation, Jameson, Morris and Martin would have been reluctant to ride very far away from the fort into the midst of the Mexican troops for fear of capture.

7

SITIADO

On the first night of the siege a company of volunteers went out and captured some prisoners. One of them was a Mexican soldier, and all through the siege he interpreted the Mexican bugle calls and in that way the defenders were warned about the movements of the enemy.

On Wednesday, 24 February, Colonel Almonte stated: 'Very early this morning a new battery was commenced on the bank of the river, about 350 yards from the Alamo. It was finished in the afternoon, and a brisk fire was kept up from it until the 18-pounder and another piece was dismounted. The President reconnoitred on horseback, passing within musket shot of the fort. According to a spy, four of the enemy were killed. At evening the music struck up, and went to entertain the enemy with it and some grenades. In the night, according to the statement of a spy, 30 men arrived at the fort from Gonzales.'

Colonel de la Pena recorded: 'On the 24th at nine o'clock His Excellency appeared and ordered that shoes be distributed in his presence among the preferred companies ...'

***

On the morning of Thursday, 25 February a Mexican unit of about three hundred men approached from the south of the Alamo using the cover of houses. They had got to within about a hundred paces when the defenders opened up a cannonade on them, supported by devastatingly accurate small arms fire, which checked them and forced them to take cover in the shacks and outhouses around the post. A party of Texians actually left the compound under fire and set fire to some of the buildings that were being used for cover by the Mexicans. After two hours the attackers retreated in disorder having sustained several casualties, while a few defenders suffered no more than cuts and bruises. During the next few days the Mexican army got closer to the ramparts by digging approach trenches and engineers constructed a series of underground bunkers that were heavily manned by troops. Their main purpose was to prevent anyone from entering or leaving the Alamo and to cut the defenders off from natural water supplies.

Colonel Almonte wrote in his diary for that day:

> The firing from our batteries was commenced early. The General-in-Chief, with the battalion of de Cazadores, crossed the river and posted themselves in the Alamo. That is to say, in the houses near the fort. A new fortification was commenced by us near the house of McMullen. In the random firing the enemy wounded four of the Cazadores de Matamoros battalion, and two of the battalion of Jimenese; and killed one corporal and a soldier of the battalion of Matamoros.
>
> Our fire ceased in the afternoon. In the night two batteries were erected by us on the other side of the river in the Alameda of the Alamo – the battalion of Matamoros was also posted there, and the cavalry was posted on the hills to the east of the enemy, and in the road from Gonzales at the Casa Mata Antigua. At half past eleven at night we retired. The enemy, in the night, burnt the straw and wooden houses in their vicinity, but did not attempt to set fire with their guns to those in our rear. A strong north wind commenced at nine at night.

Colonel de la Pena stated: 'On the 25th at nine-thirty, His Excellency appeared at the battery and had the column of Chasseurs and the battalion of Matamoros march to the other side of the San Antonio River, he himself following. Our soldiers fought within pistol range against the walls of the Alamo, and we lost two dead and six wounded.

'During the night some construction was undertaken to protect the line that had been established at the small nearby village of La Villita under orders of Colonel Morales.'

In his 'Headquarters, Fort of the Alamo' letter, Colonel Travis stated:

> Today [25 February] at 10 o'clock a.m. some two or three hundred Mexicans crossed the river below and came up under cover of the houses until they arrived within virtual point blank shot, when we opened a heavy discharge of grape and canister on them, together with a well-directed fire from small arms which forced them to halt and take shelter in the houses about 90 or 100 yards from our batteries. The action continued to rage about two hours, when the enemy retreated in confusion, dragging many of their dead and wounded.
>
> During the action, the enemy kept up a constant bombardment and discharge of balls, grape, and canister. We know from actual observation that many of the enemy were wounded – while we, on our part, have not lost a man. Two or three of our men have been slightly scratched by pieces of rock, but have not been disabled. I take great pleasure in

stating that both officers and men conducted themselves with firmness and bravery.

Lieutenant Simmons of cavalry acting as infantry, and Captains Carey, Dickinson and Blair of the artillery, rendered essential service, and Charles Despallier and Robert Brown gallantly sallied out and set fire to houses which afforded the enemy shelter, in the face of enemy fire. Indeed, the whole of the men who were brought into action conducted themselves with such heroism that it would be injustice to discriminate. The Hon. David Crockett was seen at all points, animating the men to do their duty.

For Friday, 26 February, Colonel Almonte wrote:

The northern wind continued very strong; the thermometer fell to 39, and during the rest of the day remained at 60. At daylight, there was a slight skirmish between the enemy and a small party of the division of the east, under the command of General Sesma. During the day the firing from our cannon was continued. The enemy did not reply, except now and then. At night the enemy burnt the small houses near the parapet of the battalion of San Luis, on the other side of the river. Some sentinels were advanced. In the course of the day the enemy sallied out for wood and water, and were opposed by our marksmen. The norther wind continues.

On the same day Sergeant Loranca remembered:

Santa Anna then ordered a parley to be sounded which was answered by the chiefs of the Alamo, and the President commissioned the Mexican Colonel Batres to confer with Bowie and Travis, both colonels of the Texan forces holding the Alamo. This was on 26th of February 1836.

The President Santa Anna proposed to Travis and Bowie that they should surrender at discretion, with no other guarantee than that their lives should be spared. The said Texan chiefs answered and proposed to surrender the fort on being allowed to march out with their arms and go to join their government (as they had permitted the Mexican forces under Generals Cos and Filisola when they capitulated to the Texans at the Mission de la Espada and were allowed to march out with their arms, munitions of war, provisions, etc, and join the Mexican army then in the field against Texas), and if this was not willingly conceded to them, they would willingly take all the chances of war.

***

Colonel Almonte described Saturday, 27 February as: 'The northern wind was strong at day break, and continued all the night. Thermometer at 39. Lieutenant Manuel Menchacho [of the noted Menchacho family of San Antonio] was sent with a party of men for the corn, cattle, and hogs at the Ranchos (small farms) of Seguin and Flores. It was determined to cut off the water from the enemy on the side next to the old mill. There was little firing from either side during the day. The enemy worked hard to repair some entrenchments. In the afternoon the President was observed by the enemy and fired at. In the night a courier extraordinary was dispatched to the city of Mexico, informing the Government of the taking of Bexar, and also to Generals Urrea, Filisola, Cos and Vital Fernandez. No private letters were sent.'

***

Colonel Almonte described Sunday, 28 February: 'The weather abated somewhat. The thermometer was at 40 degrees at 7:00 am. News was received that reinforcements to the enemy was coming by the road from La Bahia in number 200. It was not true. The cannonading was continued.'

The news of reinforcements was indeed true. After Colonel James Fannin heard about the despatches from Colonel Travis in Goliad, he decided to get together a relief force, and by 28 February he began the 90-mile march to San Antonio with three hundred men and four artillery pieces. However, the relief mission was a failure. The troops, many of them by then barefooted, had barely crossed the San Antonio River when the wagons began to break down; provisions were running out and oxen teams wandered off during the night.

Colonel Travis's second letter was received by Governor Henry Smith at San Filipe on 27 February 1836, who wrote the following strong stirring words:

Fellow citizens and countrymen: The foregoing official communication from Colonel Travis, now in command at Bexar, needs no comment. The garrison, composed of only 150 Americans, engaged in a deadly conflict with 1,000 of the mercenary troops of the Dictator, who are daily receiving reinforcements, should be a sufficient call upon you without saying more. However, secure, however fortunate, our garrison may be, they have not the provisions nor ammunition to stand more than a thirty days' siege at farthest. I call upon you as an officer, I implore you as a man, to fly to the aid of your besieged countrymen and not permit them to be massacred by a mercenary foe. I slight none! The call is upon ALL who are able to bear arms, to rally without one moment's delay, or in fifteen days the heart of Texas will be the seat of war. This is not imaginary. The enemy from 6,000 to 8,000 strong are on our border and rapidly moving by forced marches for the colonies. The campaign has commenced. We must promptly meet the enemy or all will be lost. Do you possess honor? Suffer it not to be insulted or tarnished. Do you possess patriotism? Evince it by your bold, prompt and manly action! If you possess even humanity you will rally without a moment's delay to the aid of your besieged countrymen!

***

Colonel Almonte recorded for Monday, 29 February: 'The weather changed – thermometer at 55 – in the night it commenced blowing hard from the west. In the afternoon the battalion of Allende took post at the east of the Alamo. The President reconnoitred. One of our soldiers was killed in the night. The wind changed to the north at midnight. About that time General Sesma left the camp with the cavalry of Dolores and the infantry of Allende to meet the enemy coming from La Bahia or Goliad to the aid of the Alamo. General Castrillon on guard.'

The Mexicans continued to tunnel nearer to the Alamo defences, and by 29 February the Allende Battalion was stationed on the east side of the defences, while the Jimenez Battalion guarded the left, along the road to Gonzales. According to Alamo survivor Enrique Espraza, there was supposed to have been a ceasefire, but Colonel de la Pena quoted information he must have read in the adjutant's logbook of the San Luis Battalion: 'On the 29th the siege continued, and about seven thirty at night the enemy killed a first class private belonging to the first company of the San Luis Battalion, Secundino Alvarez, who on orders of the president had got in close in order to reconnoitre the Alamo.'

***

Colonel Almonte reported for Tuesday, 1 March:

The wind subsided, but the weather continued cold – thermometer at 36 in the morning – day clear. Early in the morning General Sesma wrote from the Mission de la Espador that there was no such enemy, and that he reconnoitred as far as the Tinaja, without finding any traces of them. The cavalry returned to camp, and the infantry to this city. At 12 o'clock the President went out to reconnoitre the mill site to the north west of the Alamo. Lt Colonel Ampudia was commissioned to construct more trenches. In the afternoon the enemy fired two 12-pound shots at the house of the President, one of which struck the house, and the other passed it. Nothing more of consequence occurred. The night was cold, thermometer 34 Fahrenheit and 1 Reaumur.

In response to the note Travis had sent to Gonzales, Byrd Lockhart, a Texan courier and scout, was requested to muster a relief force, and on 23 February Captain Albert Martin set off with a thirty-two-man unit that was named the Gonzales Ranging Company of Volunteers; the last reinforcements to enter the Alamo.

With them was Irishman, Thomas J. Jackson, one of the 'Old Eighteen' who had confronted the Mexicans over the Gonzales cannon.

Andrew Duvalt was born in Ireland in 1804, and had been a plasterer. He had arrived in Texas from Missouri and was a resident of Gonzales. He joined Lieutenant (later Captain) Robert White's infantry company on 28 October 1835, participated in the siege of Bexar and became an infantryman in the Bexar Guards. He had returned to Gonzales by 2 February 1836, and enrolled during the muster of the Gonzales Rangers. Duvalt is listed among Gonzales residents who died at the Alamo. In 1854 his descendants received a 320-acre land bounty in recognition of his service to the Texas cause.

Marcus L. Sewell is identified as being English on a bronze plaque at the Alamo, and he is said to have been born in England in 1804. However, he is listed by several references as having been born at Jefferson in Tennessee. In both FamilySearch.org and Ancestry.com there are records of his father and mother in Tennessee; they being George Sewell and his wife Susannah (formerly Copeland). Marcus received only a limited education, and he was a shoemaker by trade. He travelled to Texas by way of New Orleans, and settled in Gonzales. He rode to San Antonio with the Gonzales Ranging Company.

Also with the unit was Charles Joseph Despallier, a 24-year-old from Louisiana. His older brother, Blaz Phillippe, had taken part in the siege of Bexar with the New Orleans Greys, but he became ill and returned to Louisiana; and another older brother, Victor Madison, was a friend of James Bowie, and acted as his attorney. Charles reached San Antonio in mid-February, but he had left the garrison on 25 February as a courier.

The Gonzales Ranging Company of Volunteers arrived at the Alamo at 1am on the morning of 1 March, having managed to get through the Mexican lines. Doctor Sutherland reported:

> So soon as we entered the town [Gonzales] we made known our mission and sent notice to all the neighbouring settlements with the news of the enemy's arrival, calling upon the citizens to come immediately to the relief of the besieged. This was on Wednesday, the twenty-fourth. By Saturday we succeeded in getting twenty-five men who were placed under the command of Ensign [George C.] Kimble. These were principally from the town of Gonzales, men of families of her best citizens. They started for San Antonio on Saturday about two o'clock pm, with John W. Smith acting as guide. On the Cibolo they increased their force to thirty-two, which number reached Bexar about one o'clock am on Tuesday, March the first.

Doctor Sutherland added:

> On reaching the suburbs of the city they were approached by a man on horseback who asked in English:
> 'Do you wish to go into the fort, gentlemen?'
> 'Yes,' was the reply.
> 'Then follow me,' said he, at the same time turning his horse into the lead of the company.
> Smith remarked, 'Boys, it's time to be after shooting that fellow.'
> When he put his spurs to his horse, sprung into the thicket, and was out of sight in a moment, before a gun could be got to bear on him. Some supposed this was General Woll, who was a French-born man in the Mexican service.
> The little band proceeded silently in single file towards the fort, but were soon to be saluted again, though not in so friendly a manner. Notwithstanding, Smith had taken the precaution to despatch a messenger ahead, there seems to have been some misunderstanding as to the direction from which they should approach the walls, for the sentinel not being aware of their presence, fired upon them without hailing. The ball took effect in the foot of one of the men. The mistake was soon rectified, when all went in without further mishap.

General Adrian Woll (1795–1875) was born near Paris, and was serving as Santa Anna's quartermaster general at the time. However, some sources state that he did not reach San Antonio until 8 March, after the battle of the Alamo.

***

For Wednesday, 2 March Colonel Almonte recorded:

> The weather commenced clear and pleasant thermometer 34 – no wind. An aide of Colonel Duque arrived with despatches from Arroyo Hondo, dated 1st inst. In reply, he was ordered to leave the river Medina, and arrive the next day at 12 or 1 o'clock. General J. Ramirez came to breakfast with the President. Information was received that there was corn at the farm of Sequin, and Lieutenant [Antonio] Menchacho was sent with a party for it. The President discovered, in the afternoon, a covered road within pistol shot of the Alamo, and posted the battalion of Jimenes there. At 5:00am Bringas went out to meet Gaona.

While still on the march towards Bexar, Colonel de la Pena recorded '… on the 2nd March a chasseur from San Luis, Trinidad Geldago, drowned, and on the 3rd my battalion along with other sapper battalions from Aldama and Toluca arrived.'

Reuben Marmaduke Potter (1802–90), who took the opportunity to interview many members of the Mexican forces for their recollections of the battle, stated:

On the 2nd of March, 1836, the delegates of the people of Texas in general convention at Washington on the Brazos declared their independence of Mexico. On the same day General Samuel Houston, the Texan commander-in-chief, issued a proclamation announcing that war was waging on the frontier, and Bexar besieged by 2,000 of the enemy, while the garrison was only 150 strong. "The citizens of Texas must rally to the aid of our army, or it will perish. Independence is declared: it must be maintained. Immediate action, united with valour, alone can achieve the great work." – But the immediate action was too late.

Following are the details of the Unanimous Declaration of Independence by the Delegation of the People of Texas, in general convention, at the town of Washington, on the Second day of March 1836:

When a government has ceased to protect the lives, liberty and property of the people, from whom its legitimate powers are derived, and for the advancement of whose happiness it was instituted, and so far from being a guarantee for the enjoyment of those inestimable and inalienable rights, becomes an instrument in the hands of evil rulers for their oppression.

When the Federal Republican Constitution of their country, which they have sworn to support, no longer has a substantial existence, and the whole nature of their government has been forcibly changed, without their consent, from a restricted federative republic, composed of sovereign states, to a consolidated central military despotism, in which every interest is disregarded but that of the army and the priesthood, both the eternal enemies of civil liberty, the ever-ready minions of power, and the usual instruments of tyrants.

When, long after the spirit of the constitution has departed, moderation is at length so far lost by those in power, that even the semblance of freedom is removed, and the forms themselves of the constitution discontinued, and so far from their petitions and remonstrances being regarded, the agents who bear them are thrown into dungeons, and mercenary armies sent forth to force a new government upon them at the point of the bayonet.

When, in consequence of such acts of malfeasance and abdication on the part of the government, anarchy prevails, and civil society is dissolved into its original elements. In such a crisis, the first law of nature, the right of self-preservation, the inherent and inalienable rights of the people to appeal to first principles, and take their political affairs into their own hands in extreme cases, enjoins it as a right towards themselves, and a sacred obligation to their posterity, to abolish such government, and create another in its stead, calculated to rescue them from impending dangers, and to secure their future welfare and happiness.

Nations, as well as individuals, are amenable for their acts to the public opinion of mankind. A statement of a part of our grievances is therefore submitted to an impartial world, in justification of the hazardous but unavoidable step now taken, of severing our political connection with the Mexican people, and assuming an independent attitude among the nations of the earth.

The Mexican government, by its colonisation laws, invited and induced the Anglo-American population of Texas to colonise its wilderness under the pledged faith of a written constitution, that they should continue to enjoy that constitutional liberty and republican government to which they had been habituated in the land of their birth, the United States of America.

In this expectation they have been cruelly disappointed, inasmuch as the Mexican nation has acquiesced in the late changes made in the government by General Antonio Lopez de Santa Anna, who having overturned the constitution of his country, now offers us the cruel alternative, either to abandon our homes, acquired by so many privations, or submit to the most intolerable of all tyranny, the combined despotism of the sword and the priesthood.

It has sacrificed our welfare to the state of Coahuila, by which our interests have been continually depressed through a jealous and partial course of legislation, carried on at a far distant seat of government, by a hostile majority, in an unknown tongue, and this too, notwithstanding we have petitioned in the humblest terms for the establishment of a separate state government, and have, in accordance with the provisions of the national constitution, presented to the general Congress a republican constitution, which was, without just cause, contemptuously rejected.

It incarcerated in a dungeon, for a long time, one of our citizens, for no other cause but a zealous endeavour to procure the acceptance of our constitution, and the establishment of a state government.

It has failed and refused to secure, on a firm basis, the right of trial by jury, that palladium of civil liberty, and only safe guarantee for the life, liberty, and property of the citizen.

It has failed to establish any public system of education, although possessed of almost boundless resources, (the public domain,) and although it is an axiom in political science, that unless a people are educated and enlightened, it is idle to expect the continuance of civil liberty, or the capacity for self government.

It has suffered the military commandants, stationed among us, to exercise arbitrary acts of oppression and tyranny, thus trampling upon the most sacred rights of the citizens, and rendering the military superior to the civil power.

It has dissolved, by force of arms, the state Congress of Coahuila and Texas, and obliged our representatives to fly for their lives from the seat of government, thus depriving us of the fundamental political right of representation.

It has demanded the surrender of a number of our citizens, and ordered military detachments to seize and carry them into the Interior for trial, in contempt of the civil authorities, and in defiance of the laws and the constitution.

It has made piratical attacks upon our commerce, by commissioning foreign desperadoes, and authorizing them to seize our vessels, and convey the property of our citizens to far distant ports for confiscation.

It denies us the right of worshipping the Almighty according to the dictates of our own conscience, by the support of a national religion, calculated to promote the temporal interest of its human functionaries, rather than the glory of the true and living God.

It has demanded us to deliver up our arms, which are essential to our defence, the rightful property of freemen, and formidable only to tyrannical governments.

It has invaded our country both by sea and by land, with intent to lay waste our territory, and drive us from our homes; and has now a large mercenary army advancing, to carry on against us a war of extermination.

It has, through its emissaries, incited the merciless savage, with the tomahawk and scalping knife, to massacre the inhabitants of our defenceless frontiers.

It hath been, during the whole time of our connection with it, the contemptible sport and victim of successive military revolutions, and hath continually exhibited every characteristic of a weak, corrupt, and tyrannical government.

These, and other grievances, were patiently borne by the people of Texas, until they reached that point at which forbearance ceases to be a virtue. We then took up arms in defence of the national constitution. We appealed to our Mexican brethren for assistance. Our appeal has been made in vain. Though months have elapsed, no sympathetic response has yet been heard from the Interior.

We are, therefore, forced to the melancholy conclusion, that the Mexican people have acquiesced in the destruction of their liberty, and the substitution therefore of a military government; that they are unfit to be free, and incapable of self government.

The necessity of self-preservation, therefore, now decrees our eternal political separation.

We, therefore, the delegates with plenary powers of the people of Texas, in solemn convention assembled, appealing to a candid world for the necessities of our condition, do hereby resolve and declare, that our political connection with the Mexican nation has forever ended, and that the people of Texas do now constitute a free, Sovereign, and independent republic, and are fully invested with all the rights and attributes which properly belong to independent nations; and, conscious of the rectitude of our intentions, we fearlessly and confidently commit the issue to the decision of the Supreme arbiter of the destinies of nations.

It was then signed by the President, Richard Ellis, and all the other delegates who were present.

***

On Thursday, 3 March Major Bonham returned to the Alamo, bearing through the Mexican lines with a letter from Judge Robert McAlpine Williamson (1804–59), a major in the Texas Rangers, assuring Travis that help was on its way and urging him to hold out.

Mrs Dickinson stated: 'Colonel Crockett was a performer on the violin, and often during the siege took it up and played his favourite tunes. I heard him say several times during the eleven days of the siege: "I think we had better march out and die in the open air. I don't like being hemmed-up." There were provisions and forage enough in the fort to have subsisted men and horses for a month longer.'

On that same day Colonel Travis wrote three letters, and all three were taken out by James L. Allen on 5 March. One was to the President of the Convention from the Commandancy of the Alamo, Bejar:

In the present confusion of the political authorities of the country, and in the absence of the commander-in-chief, I beg leave to communicate to you the situation of this garrison. You have doubtless already seen my official report of the 25th ult. made on that day to General Sam Houston, together with the various communications heretofore sent by express. I shall, therefore, confine myself to what has transpired since that date.

From the 25th to the present date, the enemy have kept up a bombardment from two howitzers (one a five and a half inch, and the other an eight inch) and a heavy cannonade from two long nine-pounders, mounted on a battery on the opposite side of the river, at a distance of four hundred yards from our walls. During this period the enemy has been busily employed in encircling us with entrenchments on all sides, at the following distance, to within Bexar, four hundred yards west; in La Villeta, three hundred yards south; at the powder-house, one thousand yards east by south; on the ditch, eight hundred yards north.

Notwithstanding all this, a company of thirty-two men from Gonzales made their way into us on the morning of the 1st inst, at three o'clock, and Col. J.B. Bonham (a courier from Gonzales) got in this morning [3 March] at eleven o'clock without molestation.

In his letter to Jesse Grimes he confirmed that Bonham had got through the Mexican lines by way of coming between the powder house to the south-east of Bexar and the Mexican upper encampment:

> I have so fortified this place, that the walls are generally proof against cannon-balls; and I shall continue to entrench on the inside, and strengthen the walls by throwing up dirt. At least two hundred shells have fallen inside our works without having injured a single man; indeed, we have been so fortunate as not to lose a man from any cause, and we have killed many of the enemy. The spirits of my men are still high, although they have had much to depress them. We have contended for ten days against an enemy whose numbers are variously estimated at from fifteen hundred to six thousand, with Gen. Ramirez Sesma and Col. Bartres, the aid-de-camp of Santa Anna, at their head. A report was circulated that Santa Anna himself was with the enemy, but I think it was false.
>
> A reinforcement of one thousand men is now entering Bexar from the west, and I think it more than probable that Santa Anna is now in town, from the rejoicing we hear. Col. Fannin is said to be on the march to this place with reinforcements; but I fear it is not true, as I have repeatedly sent to him for aid without receiving any. Col. Bonham, my special messenger, arrived at Labahia fourteen days ago, with a request for aid; and on the arrival of the enemy in Bexar ten days ago, I sent an express to Col. F. which arrived at Goliad on the next day, urging him to send us reinforcements – none have arrived. I look to the colonies alone for aid; unless it arrives soon, I shall have to fight the enemy on his own terms. I will, however, do the best I can under the circumstances, and I feel confident that the determined valour and desperate courage, heretofore evinced by my men, will not fail them in the last struggle, and although they may be sacrificed to the vengeance of a Gothic enemy, the victory will cost the enemy so dear, that it will be worse for him than a defeat. I hope your honourable body will hasten on reinforcements, ammunition, and provisions to our aid, as soon as possible. We have provisions for twenty days for the men we have; our supply of ammunition is limited. At least five hundred pounds of cannon powder, and two hundred rounds of six, nine, twelve, and eighteen pound balls – ten kegs of rifle powder, and a supply of lead, should be sent to this place without delay, under a sufficient guard.
>
> If these things are promptly sent, and large reinforcements are hastened to this frontier, this neighbourhood will be the great and decisive battle ground. The power of Santa Anna is to be met here or in the colonies; we had better meet them here, than to suffer a war of desolation to rage our settlements. A blood-red banner waves from the church of Bexar, and in the camp above us, in token that the war is one of vengeance against rebels; they have declared us as such, and demanded

that we should surrender at discretion or this garrison should be put to the sword. Their threats have had no influence on me or my men, but to make all fight with desperation, and that high-souled courage which characterises the patriot, who is willing to die in defence of his country's liberty and his own honour.

The citizens of this municipality are all our enemies except those who have joined us heretofore; we have but three Mexicans now in the fort; those who have not joined us in this extremity, should be declared public enemies, and their property should aid in paying the expenses of the war.

The bearer of this will give you your honourable body, a statement more in detail, should he escape through the enemy's lines. God and Texas! Victory or Death!

P.S. The enemy's troops are still arriving, and the reinforcements will probably amount to two or three thousand.

The new Texas government commissioned a printer in San Filipe to produce one thousand copies of the letter, and Texas patriots delivered them all over the country in an effort to inspire fagging spirits among the Texans.

James L. Allen also carried some letters from other defenders, one of them thought to have been written by Isaac Millsaps, a 41-year-old from Tennessee, who had arrived with the Gonzales Relief Force two days earlier, and whose blind wife and as many as seven children lived in Gonzales. It is considered to be a forgery; some of the reasons being that all the information contained in it was known at the time it was discovered in the early 1960s, and it gives little detail concerning his family. However, it could have been forged from an original letter, no ion-diffusion analysis has been carried out on the document, a process that can prove if it is authentic or not, and I personally believe the signature on the letter does resemble one that is thought to be authentic. What is known for sure is that Isaac Millsap lost his life at the Alamo. I believe the contents warrant inclusion here for consideration, and for the reader to decide. I have included some editing for clarity:

We are in the fortress of the Alamo, a ruined church that has most fell down. The Mexicans are here in large numbers. They have kept up a constant fire since we got here. All our boys are well and Captain Martin is in good spirits.

Early this morning I watched the Mexicans drilling just out of range. They was marching up and down with such order. They have bright red and blue uniforms and many cannon. Some here at this place believe that the main army has not come up yet. I think they is all here, even Santa Anna.

Colonel Bowie is down sick and had to be to bed. I saw him yesterday and he is still ready to fight. He didn't know me from last spring but did remember Wash. He tells all that help will be here soon, and it makes us feel good.

We have beef and corn to eat but no coffee. The bag I had fell off on the way here so it was all spilt.

I have not seen Travis, but the times since here. He told us all this morning that Fanning was going to be here early with more men and there would be a good fight. He stays on the wall some, but mostly to his room.

I hope help comes soon cause we can't fight them all. Some says he is going to talk some tonight and group us better for defence. If we fail here get to the river with the children; all Texas will be before the enemy. We get so little news here, we know nothing. There is no discontent in our boys. Some are tired from loss of sleep and rest. The Mexicans are shooting every few minutes but most of the shots fall inside and do no harm. I don't know what else to say, they is calling for all letters.

Kiss the dear children for me, and believe as I do that all will be well, and God protects us all – Isaac.

If any men come through these tell them to hurry with powder for it is short. I hope you get this, and know – I love you all.

For 3 March Colonel Almonte recorded:

The weather commenced clear, at 40 without wind. The enemy fired a few cannon and musket shots at the city. I wrote to Mexico and to my sister, directed them to send their letters to Bexar, and that before three months the campaign would be ended. The General-in-Chief went out to reconnoitre. A battery was erected on the north of the Alamo within musket shot. Official despatches were received from General Urrea, announcing that he had routed the colonists at San Patricio – killing 16 and taking 21 prisoners. The bells were rung. The battalion of Zapadores, Almada, and Toluca arrived. The enemy attempted a sally in the night at the Sugar Mill, but were repulsed by our advance.

These three battalions from the 1st Brigade were under General Cos, consisting of about 900 troops, with about 150 mule herders, making a grand total of Mexican forces at San Antonio of about 2,500.

By returning to Bexar General Cos was violating the first stipulation of his capitulation by which he and his officers were permitted to retire with their arms and private property into the interior of the Mexican Republic – 'Under parole of honor that they would not in any way oppose the re-establishment of the Federal Constitution of 1824'.

The reinforcements consisted of Colonel de la Pena's 185 *Zapadores* (assault engineers), along with Colonel Amat, who was second in command, Colonel Castaneda with 393 men of the Aldama *Permanente* Regiment, and Colonel Duque, who brought in 324 men of the Toluca *Activo* Battalion.

Also with the Toluca Battalion was a *soldado* named Sergeant Felix Nunez. He stated that he was born in 1804 and had been forcibly conscripted into the army in the Guadalajara *Activo* Battalion. This battalion was always under the command of Santa Anna, and although it fought during the Texas revolution it did not take part in the San Antonio campaign.

In his 1875 *History of Texas*, James Morphis relates to a story left by a man named Louis 'Moses' Rose, who it states left the Alamo on 3 March. The story had appeared in the *Texas Almanac* two years earlier:

> The following account of an escape from the Alamo is from a late Texas publication, and may throw more light upon the last hours of its immortal defenders. About two hours before sunset, on the third day of March, 1836, the bombardment suddenly ceased, and the enemy withdrew an unusual distance. Taking advantage of that opportunity, Colonel Travis paraded all of his effective men in a single file; and, taking his position in front of the centre, he stood for some moments, apparently speechless from emotion. Then, nerving himself for the occasion, he addressed them substantially as follows:
>
> 'I must now speak of our present situation. Here we are, surrounded by an army that could almost eat us for a breakfast, from whose arms our lives are for the present protected by the stone walls. We have no hope of help, for no force that we could ever reasonably have expected could cut its way through the strong ranks of these Mexicans. We dare not surrender; for, should we do so, that black flag, now waving in our sight, as well as the merciless character of our enemies, admonishes us of what would be our doom. We cannot cut our way out through the enemy's ranks; for, in attempting that, we should all be slain in less than ten minutes. Nothing remains then, but to stay within this fort and fight to the last moment. In this case, we must, sooner or later, all be slain; for I am sure that Santa Anna is determined to storm the fort and take it, even at the greatest cost of the lives of his own men.
>
> 'Then we must die! Our speedy dissolution is a fixed and inevitable fact. Our business is, not to make a fruitless effort to save our lives, but to choose the manner of our death. But three modes are presented to us. Let us choose that by which we may best serve our country. Shall we surrender, and be deliberately shot, without taking the life of a single enemy? Shall we try to cut our way out through the Mexican ranks, and be butchered before we can kill twenty of our adversaries? I am opposed

to either method; for, in either case, we could but lose our lives without benefiting our friends at home – our fathers and mothers, our brothers and sisters, our wives and little ones. The Mexican army is strong enough to march through the country, and exterminate its inhabitants, and our countrymen are not able to oppose them in open field. My choice, then, is to remain in this fort, to resist every assault, and to sell our lives as dearly as possible.

'Then let us band together as brothers, and vow to die together. Let us resolve to withstand our adversaries to the last; and, at each advance, to kill as many of them as possible. And when, at last, they shall storm our fortress, let us kill them as they come! kill them as they scale our wall! kill them as they leap within! kill them as they raise their weapons, and as they use them! kill them as they kill our companions! and continue to kill them as long as one of us shall remain alive!

'By this policy, I trust that we shall so weaken our enemies that our countrymen at home can meet them on fair terms, cut them up, expel them from the country, and thus establish our own independence, and secure prosperity and happiness to our families and our country. And, be assured, our memory will be gratefully cherished by posterity, till all history shall be erased, and all noble deeds shall be forgotten.

'But I leave every man to his own choice. Should any man prefer to surrender, and be tied and shot; or to attempt an escape through the Mexican ranks, and be killed before he can run a hundred yards, he is at liberty to do so.

'My own choice is to stay in this fort, and die for my country, fighting as long as breath shall remain in my body. This I will do, even if you leave me alone. Do as you think best – but no man can die with me without affording me comfort in the moment of death.'

Colonel Travis then drew his sword, and with its point traced a line upon the ground, extending from the right to the left of the file. Then, resuming his position in front of the centre, he said:

'I now want every man who is determined to stay here and die with me to come across this line. Who will be first? March!'

The first respondent was Tapley Holland [of Carey's Artillery], who leaped the line at a bound, exclaiming, 'I am ready to die for my country!'

His example was instantly followed by every man in the file, with the exception of Rose. Manifest enthusiasm was universal and tremendous. Every sick man that could walk arose from his bunk and tottered across the line. Colonel Bowie, who could not leave his bed, said, 'Boys, I am not able to come to you, but I wish some of you would be so kind as to remove my cot over there.' Four men instantly ran to the cot, and, each lifting a corner carried it across the line. Then every sick man that could not walk made the same request, and had his bunk removed in like manner.

Rose, too, was deeply affected, but differently from his companions. He stood till every man but himself had crossed the line. A consciousness of the real situation overpowered him. He sank upon the ground,

The Alamo chapel became known as 'The Shrine of Texas Liberty' - and a memorial to the Alamo defenders.

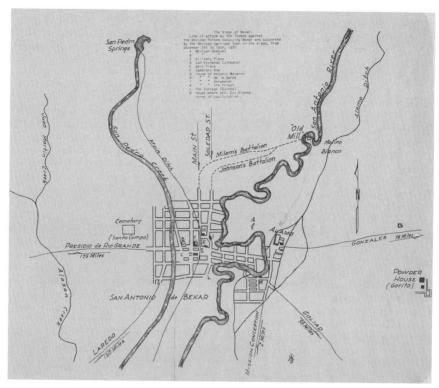

A map of Bexar dated from about the time of the centenary, showing the line of the two-pronged attack made by the Texans against Mexican forces occupying Bexar. It shows the layout of San Antonio de Bexar and the Alamo, including roads, major buildings, rivers and creeks. Some modern streets of San Antonio have been superimposed onto the map.

A view of the San Antonio River looking west from the area of the Alamo complex towards the San Fernando Church.

The Veramendi Palace on Soledad Street in Bexar was the scene of several historic events. It was the house of James Bowie's in-laws where his marriage to Ursula Veramendi is said to have taken place in 1831, and where Colonel Ben Milam was killed in action during the siege of Bexar.

'Cos House' in about 1922, which still exists in La Villita ('the Little Village'), south-west of the Alamo. It was here that General Cos had his headquarters, and where the document for the capitulation of Bexar was signed.

The flag of the New Orleans Greys that was captured during the battle of the Alamo and is now on display at the Natural History Museum in Mexico City. The Americans have offered three Mexican flags that had been captured at San Jacinto in an exchange to bring the flag back to Texas. Mexico has refused the offer, and sometimes they do not admit they even have it in their possession.

Crockett Street Bridge, which was no more than a footbridge at the time of the siege, is where Captain Martin met Colonel Almonte under a flag of truce on 23 February 1836.

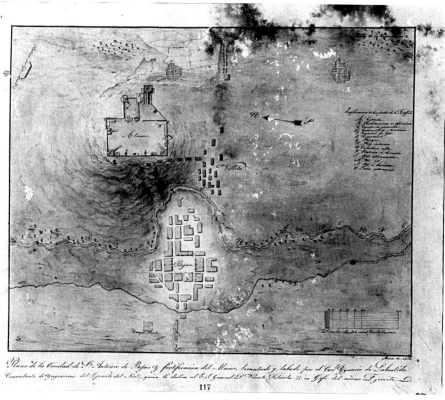

The map prepared by Santa Anna's Commander of Engineers, Ignacio de Labastida. The plan shows one footbridge across the San Antonio River, situated about where the bridge is on East Crockett Street. There is no crossing at the place where East Commerce Street is today, which is further around the bend of the river.

Gonzales was a settlement about 60 miles to the east of San Antonio. It was here where the first incident in the Texas Revolution occurred, and from where the last men set out to reinforce the Alamo garrison.

Nacogdoches was a busy cattle market town, where several of the men who lost their lives at the Alamo had settled prior to the revolution. The New Orleans Greys bivouacked there on their way to Bexar, where they received a banquet in their honour. There are two memorials dedicated to the unit in the town.

A painting of the Alamo complex and some of the fighting by a Parisian artist named Jean Louis Theodore Gentilz (1819–1906). The scale is not accurate, but he spoke to some of the eyewitnesses and had access to the Alamo ruins before they were rebuilt by United States soldiers in 1850.

A view of the interior of the Alamo mission looking towards the door, which was taken in about 1904. The photograph gives an idea of how sturdy the building is, and the rooms to the far right of the picture are probably where the gunpowder was stored, and the non-combatants hid as the fighting raged outside.

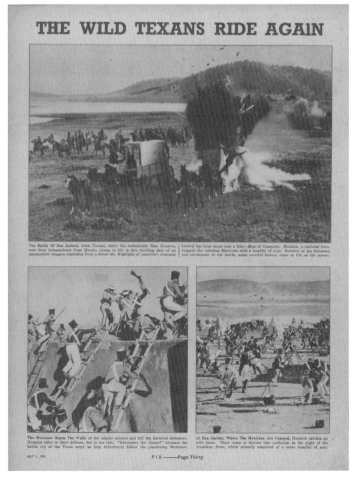

A page from *PIX* magazine of 30 June 1939, depicting images from the recent film about Sam Houston *Man of Conquest*, which received three Academy Award nominations.

A panoramic view of the Alamo in about 1930, showing the chapel front to the right and the long barracks in the foreground. The complex is almost surrounded by Ford cars.

The memorial dedicated to the New Orleans Greys situated at Sterne House in Nacogdoches, where the unit stayed for a short time on their way to Bexar.

At the time of the centenary in 1936, the defenders buried in the sanctuary of the Old San Fernando Church were exhumed and exposed to public view for a year. Two years later they were entombed in a marble coffin, and on the same day a memorial plaque was erected in the church that records the events.

'The Spirit of Sacrifice' Alamo Cenotaph was built at the time of the centenary in San Antonio adjacent to the front of the chapel.

covered his face, and yielded to his own reflections. For a time he was unconscious of what was transpiring around him. A bright idea came to his relief; he spoke the Mexican dialect very fluently, and could he once get safely out of the fort, he might easily pass for a Mexican and effect an escape. Thus encouraged, he suddenly aroused as if from sleep. He looked over the area of the fort; every sick man's berth was at its wonted place; every effective soldier was at his post, as if awaiting orders; he felt as if dreaming. He directed a searching glance at the cot of Colonel Bowie. There lay his gallant friend. Colonel David Crockett was leaning over the cot, conversing with its occupant in an undertone. After a few seconds Bowie looked at Rose and said, 'You seem not to be willing to die with us, Rose?'

'No,' said Rose, 'I am not prepared to die, and shall not do so if I can avoid it.'

Then Crockett also looked at him, and said, 'You may as well conclude to die with us, old man, for escape is impossible.'

Rose made no reply, but looked up at the top of the wall.

'I have often done worse than to climb that wall,' thought he. Suiting the action to the thought he sprang up, seized his wallet of unwashed clothes, and ascended the wall. Standing on its top, he looked down within to take a last view of his dying friends. They were all now in motion, but what they were doing he heeded not. Overpowered by his feelings he looked away and saw them no more.

The writer takes this account of Mr Rose, *cum qrano salis*, but it may be true.

Louis Rose (1785–1850), a sawmill worker living in Nacogdoches, is said to have told this story to the parents of William Physick Zuber, who in turn told it to the *Texas Almanac* in 1873. After escaping the Mexican army camped around the garrison he is said to have turned up at the Zuber farm in March 1836 with bloodstained clothes and infected wounds, stating that he had escaped from the Alamo.

***

Colonel Almonte wrote of Friday, 4 March:

The day commenced windy, but not cold – thermometer 42. We commenced firing very early, which the enemy did not return. In the afternoon one or two shots were fired by them.

A meeting of Mexican generals and colonels was held, at which General Cos, Sesma and Castrillon were present (Generals Amador and Ventura Mora did not attend – the former having been suspended, and the latter being in active commission). Also present were Colonels Francisco Duque of Toluca, Orishuela of battalion Almada, Romero of

Battalion of Matamoros; Amat of Battalion Zapadores; and the Major of the Battalion of San Luis. The colonels of Battalion Jimenes and San Luis did not attend, being engaged in actual commission. I was also called.

After a long conference, Cos, Castrillion, Orishuela and Romero were of the opinion that the Alamo should be assaulted – first opening a breach with the two cannon and the two mortars, and that they should wait the arrival of the two 12-pounders expected on Monday, 7 March.

The President, General Ramirez and I were of the opinion that the 12-pounders should not be waited for, but the assault made. Colonels Duque and Amat, and the major of the San Luis battalion did not give any definite opinion about either of the two modes of assault proposed. In this state things remained – the General not making any definite resolution.

In the night the north parapet was advanced towards the enemy through the water course. A lieutenant of engineers conducted the entrenchment. A message was despatched to Urrea.

8

PREPARE FOR BATTLE

As each day passed the stubborn resistance of the defenders was frustrating Santa Anna and on Saturday, 5 March he held a council of war with his officers, most of whom were in favour of waiting until heavier guns could be brought into action or the defenders simply gave in from the effects of exhaustion and want of supplies, which would prevent further bloodshed. However, Santa Anna knew that if the defenders were allowed to surrender at their own will it would not enhance his reputation as a leader of fighting men. The assault would begin at first light next day – the Sabbath!

Colonel Almonte remembered: 'The day commenced very moderate – thermostat 50 – weather clear. A brisk fire was commenced from our north battery against the enemy, which was not answered, except now and then. At mid-day the thermometer rose to 68. The President determined to make the assault, and it was agreed with the commanding officers, and they came to the conclusion that they should muster at 12 o'clock tonight and at 4 o'clock tomorrow morning (Sunday, 6 March) the attack should be made.'

Colonel Amador of Santa Anna's staff, writing on the afternoon of 5 March 1836, stated:

Being necessary to act decisively upon the enemy defending the Alamo, the Most Excellent General-in-Chief has ordered that tomorrow at four o'clock the attacking columns, placed at short distance from the first trenches, will undertake the assault to begin with a special signal given by the General by means of the sounding of a bugle from the North battery.

The points from which these columns will mount their attacks will be designated by the General-in-Chief at the opportune time, and then the column commanders will receive their orders.

The men carrying the ladders will sling their rifles on their backs until the ladders are properly placed.

The companies of Grenadiers and Scouts will carry ammunition at six rounds per man and at four the riflemen, and two flints in reserves. These men will not wear cloaks, carry blankets, or anything else which will inhibit them to manoeuvre quickly.

During the day all shako chin-straps will be correctly worn – these the commanders will watch closely. The troops will wear shoes or sandals. The attacking troops will turn in after the night's prayers as they will form their columns at midnight.

The untrained recruits will remain in their camps. All armaments will be in good shape – especially bayonets.

As soon as the moon rises the riflemen of the Active Battalion, San Luis, will move back to their quarters to get their equipment ready, this will be done by leaving their stations in the line.

The Cavalry, under the command of General D Joaquin Ramirez y Sesma, will occupy the Alameda and will saddle-up at three o'clock in the morning. Their duty will be to guard the camp and keep anyone from deserting.

Take this into consideration: Against foreigners opposing us, the Honour of our Nation and army is at stake. His Supreme Excellency, the General-in-Chief, expects each man to fulfil his duties and to exert himself to give his country a day of glory and satisfaction. He well-knows how to reward those brave men who form the Army of Operations.

Overall command of the troops of the 1st Column ordered to assault the west-to-north-west walls would be led by General de Cos, with General Amador of Santa Anna's staff. Lieutenant Colonel Gregorio Urunuela would lead one battalion of 200 fusiliers and riflemen of his Aldama *Permanente* Battalion (without grenadiers), one squad being commanded by Lieutenant Castaneda, with three companies of 100 fusiliers of the 1st San Luis Potosi *Activo* (Militia) Battalion. They would carry ten scaling ladders, two crowbars and two axes. It was probably no coincidence that Santa Anna put Cos and Castenada in the same column, as they both had serious axes to grind against the Texans.

The 2nd Column of troops preparing to assault the north section was would be led by Colonel Duque. Brigadier General Castrillon and Brigadier General Amador were to lead the assault, with 130 men of the Toluca *Activo* Battalion (without grenadiers), led by Captain Jose Maria Herrera; along with three fusilier companies of the San Luis

Potosi *Activo* Battalion. They would also carry ten scaling ladders, two crowbars and two axes.

The 3rd Column of troops to the east-to-north-east section would be led by Colonel Romero, ahead of 272 men from the rifle companies of his Matamoros *Permanente* Battalion; with Colonel Mariano de Salas and his 274 men of the Jimenez *Permanente* Battalion, and men of the San Luis Potosi *Activo* Battalion. They would carry six ladders.

The 4th Column of soldiers set to assault the south ramparts would be led by Colonel Morales with 120 men of his San Luis Potosi *Activo* Battalion; while Colonel Minon was assigned to lead riflemen of the Matamoros *Permanente* Battalion, and riflemen of the Jimenez *Permanente* Battalion. They would carry only two ladders.

Santa Anna was to join the troops to the south of the Alamo at the moment of attack, which consisted of a reserve force under Colonel Amat and 185 men of his newly arrived *Zapadores* (Engineers) Battalion. Colonel de Andrade (a cavalryman), and Colonel de la Pena would lead five companies of grenadiers from the *Permanente* Battalions of Matamoros, Jimenez and Aldama, and the *Activo* Battalions of Toluca and San Luis Potosi (160 men). Also with this unit would be Colonel Labastida, who was on Santa Anna's Staff.

The cavalry consisted of 290 troopers of the Dolores *Permanente* Regiment, with elements of the Rio Grande Presidial Company, all to be led by Brigadier General Sesma. No artillery was assigned to the assault but Lieutenant Colonel Ampudia was present.

Colonel de la Pena stated:

> Once the order was issued, even those opposing it were ready to carry it out; no one doubted that we would triumph, but it was anticipated that the struggle would be bloody, as indeed it was.
>
> All afternoon of the fifth was spent in preparations. Night came, and with it the most sober reflections. Our soldiers, it was said, lacked the cool courage that is demanded by an assault, but they were steadfast and the survivors will have nothing to be ashamed of. Each one individually confronted and prepared his soul for the terrible moment, expressed his last wishes, and silently and coolly took those steps that precede an encounter. It was a general duel from which it was important to us to emerge with honour. No harangue preceded this combat, but the example given was the most eloquent language and the most absolute order.

José Juan Sánchez-Navarro's plan of the Alamo;
with descriptions translated from Spanish:

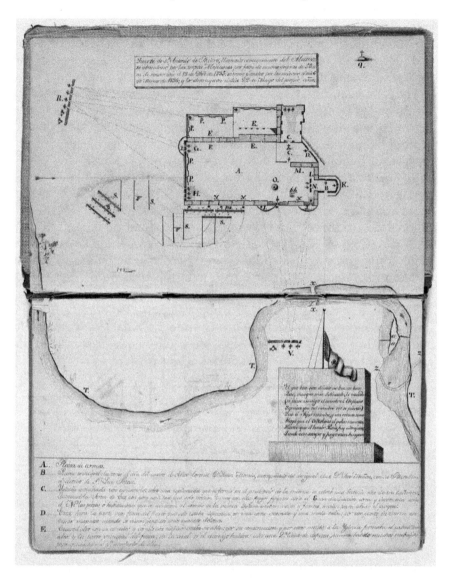

A. Parade Grounds.

B. Main gate. It was taken the day of the assault by Colonel Don Juan Morales assisted by an [officer] of the same rank, Don José Miñón, and his battalion, the reserve militia of San Luis Potosí.

C. Church in ruins, with a cemetery. On an esplanade formed in the chancel of the same, a high battery of three cannon was set up and named Fort ín de Cos. [It was] not very practical because it could be used for firing down only toward the east [and because of] a slight and cumbersome declivity toward the north. The rooms or apartments which appear on the side of the same church were strong and usable.

D. This was the weakest part of the fort since it was protected only by a short palisade and a poor barricade of trees. At this point a few colonists tried in vain to escape when they saw all was lost.

E. Tall cuartel with a corridor and a corral. This edifice was usable because of its construction and because it was contiguous to the church. It formed the high fortification and the principal part of the fort. If the enemy had made it into a second line of defence it would have been very difficult to have taken it from them or to have driven them out of it.

F. Barracks for the troops and corral for horses, through which, with the Matamoros and Ximénez Battalions, the colonel of the first [named], Don José María Romero, attacked and entered. This corral and cuartel, whose exterior wall was two feet thick and twelve feet high, were protected by the two cannon shown in their [respective] angles toward the north on esplanades one foot [high] and by embrasures.

G. Battery of two cannon called by the Mexicans Fortín de Terán located upon the wall at the height of eleven feet, Mexican vara. The wall was two feet thick; it was reinforced on the outside by a palisade with earth in between which made it five feet thick. Through the said point and through the line which runs toward the centre of the other battery, Colonel Duque attacked with his Toluca Battalion; and because he was wounded, General Castrillón continued the attack and entered the fort with the Toluca and the Zapadores [Battalions]. In the esplanade of the said battery, the commander of the colonists, named Travis, died like a soldier.

H. Through this point, called Fortín de Condelle, having the same elevation as the foregoing, General Don Martín Perfecto de Cos attempted to attack with the first column of attack composed of the Aldama *cazadores* and fusiliers and one hundred fusiliers of the reserve militia of San Luis. But having lost many men by the sustained firing by the battery and being annoyed by the firing of the Toluca Battalion, he ordered an oblique movement to the right; and since this was executed promptly and effectively, he flanked the enemy on all sides at the point which he believed the strongest; and he entered the plaza by the postern, over the wall, and by the other points marked by ***.

I. Rooms that were in the interior [side] of the wall which had loopholes for rifles toward the outside and the inside.

J. Circular saps with a moat and stockade defending the exterior of the enclosure.

K. Moat defending the main gate.

L. Hospital. In the inner room located in the fore part toward the main gate, the braggart James [Bowie] died without resisting.

M. Kitchens.

N. Barrier or trench for the defence of the gate.

O. Well dug by the colonists for water.

P. Inner moat and poorly constructed banquette with which the colonists, thinking they were reinforcing part of the fort, weakened it.

Q. Place where the bodies of two hundred fifty-seven ungrateful colonists were burned.

R. Battery for demolition and repercussion set up against the fort at [a distance of] a fusil shot, with which a breach could have been opened in two hours; but it was not ordered to go into action. It was constructed by order of General Amador under the supervision of Lieutenant Colonel Ampudia on the night of the fourth and dawn of the fifth of March. It was manned by the reserve column composed of the Zapadores Battalion and of the companies of grenadiers of the other battalions. It was commanded by His Excellency the President.

S. Position held by the first column of attack under the command of General Cos from three in the morning of the sixth of March, where they remained flat on the ground until five, when they received the signal from the trench to attack. The march and movements made by them before beginning the actual assault are shown.

T. River of San Antonio de Béxar.

V. Battery set up in the City of Béxar since the first of March.

X. Board bridge to facilitate the passage of the people from Béxar to the Alamo.

Z. Ford for vehicles and horses going toward la Villita.

aa. Island which facilitates the crossing of the river by means of two boards.

bb. Three dismounted cannon which were found within the Alamo.

A young negro named Ben, who was a cook at Santa Anna's headquarters, stated in an account of 1840:

> On the night of 7th [sic], Santa Anna ordered this servant to prepare and keep refreshments ready all night, and he stated that Santa Anna appeared cast down and discontented, and did not retire to rest at all. That, accompanied by his private secretary, the general went out about 11 o'clock and did not return until three in the morning. That he served them with coffee of which Santa Anna took but little and seemed much excited, and observed, to Almonte, that if the garrison could be induced to surrender he would be content; for he said, if they will not, I well know that every man before dawn of day must, unprepared, meet his God. But, what more can I do? My summonses, said he, are treated with disdain, it appears to me the only alternative presented is to assault the garrison, we cannot delay longer wasting the resources of the nation and any termination of the affair will relieve me of a load of anxiety. He further stated that at 4 o'clock Santa Anna and other officers left the house ...

***

There were several examples of brothers-in-arms at the Alamo. Twenty-year-old Private Edward Nelson was looking after his older brother, George, who had been wounded at Bexar while serving with Captain Thomas Breece's unit of New Orleans Greys. They were the sons of William Nelson of South Carolina. Edward had originally been in the artillery during the siege of Bexar, and he is believed to have entered the Alamo with Colonel Bowie's unit.

Although they were from Tennessee, three brothers named Edward, James and George Taylor did not arrive with Davy Crockett's men, so, as they were members of the regular Texas army, it is presumed that they probably arrived with Travis's troops. They were the sons of Anson Taylor and his wife Elizabeth; all born in Tennessee, Edward in Stewart County in 1812; and both James and George in Giles County. The story is told that the brothers were picking cotton on the farm of Captain Theodore Dorsett, in Liberty County, Round Point near Anahuac, when they heard news of the problems between the Texan settlers and the Mexican government, and others talking about forming a new government for Texas. Edward was described by Captain Dorsett's daughter, Amanda, as being a good marksman, and when the job was done they enlisted in the Texas army.

At least two defenders were cousins, they being Jacob and Asa Walker of Tennessee, and Jacob was a brother of the famous scout and mountain man Captain Joseph Rutherford Walker (1798–1876). Mrs Dickinson recalled, 'He [Jacob] spoke to me several times during the siege about his wife and four children with anxious tenderness.' The Walkers had taken part in the siege of Bexar, and Jacob, who was aged 36, was a member of Captain Carey's Artillery Company. He had left his wife, Sara Ann, and their four children in Nacogdoches. Asa was either wounded at Bexar or fell sick afterwards, and he was in hospital in the Alamo as a member of Captain Robert White's Bexar Guards.

Doctor Sutherland recorded: 'Some have supposed that Travis and his men were greatly deficient in discipline and knowledge of the art of war. That they knew little of military tactics is quite true, but that they were proficient in the use of arms were as well unsaid, as no pioneer, frontiersman ever knew anything better than how to use his arms, his daily and nightly companions. That none knew better how to handle them than the Alamo men, their work during this siege and on the 6th of March will forever attest.'

Most of the men in the garrison were weary from lack of sleep as the constant barrages of enemy fire kept them awake, and they had been on the alert from the first day of the siege. They knew that the end was near and a final assault was to be made. The feelings of isolation must have been dreadful, particularly in the face of an enemy with a leader who had a reputation for ruthlessness, and no quarter was to be given. Hearts began to pound as they realised that the only thing they could put their faith in when the final battle came was their tense and nervous comrades beside them and their own ability to defend themselves with their rifle. Thoughts of families and friends must have raced through their minds and brought sadness to their hearts to think that they may never see home again.

9

SAVAGE FURY

At dawn on the morning of Sunday, 6 March 1836, Mexican armed units approached all four walls of the Alamo ready for a final devastating assault. The infantry formed the front lines, accompanied by fatigue parties carrying the necessary equipment to breach the walls at vulnerable places. It was very cold, but they had been ordered not to wear overcoats or anything that would impede their movements. It is said that the more experienced veterans were positioned on the outside of the columns to control and guide the less experienced. The cavalry were behind them because it was considered that the clanging of the horse equipment or their snorting might warn the Texan sentinels of their approach, their officers having been given special orders to kill any infantryman who dared to lose his nerve and turn back. It is believed that General Sesma stationed his Lancers on a hill to get a panoramic view of the battlefield, where stood an abandoned powder house situated to the south-east of the Alamo, with orders to neutralise any attempt by the defenders to escape. It was a dreadful scenario of everyone involved; and it is unlikely that any man present that day was in a good state of mind – particularly Travis and Santa Anna.

Colonel de la Pena captured the mood of the situation:

> Beginning at one o'clock in the morning of the 6th, the columns were set in motion, and at three they silently advanced towards the river, which they crossed marching two abreast over some narrow wooden bridges. A few minor obstacles were explored in order to reach the enemy without being noticed, to a point personally designated by the commander-in-chief, where they stationed themselves, resting with weapons in hand. Silence was again ordered, and smoking was prohibited. The moon was up, but the density of the clouds that covered it allowed only an opaque light in our direction, seeming thus to contribute to our designs. This half-light, the silence we kept, hardly

interrupted by soft murmurs, the coolness of the morning air, the great quietude that seemed to prolong the hours, and the dangers we would soon have to face, all of this rendered our situation grave; we were still breathing and able to communicate. Within a few moments many of us would be able to answer the questions addressed to us, having already returned to nothingness whence we had come; others, badly wounded, would remain stretched out for hours without anyone thinking of them, each still fearing that perhaps an enemy cannonball whistling overhead would drop at his feet and put an end to his sufferings. Nevertheless hope stirred us, and within a few moments this anxious uncertainty would disappear; an insult to our arms had to be avenged, as well as the blood of our friends spilled three months before within these same walls we were about to attack.

Light began to appear on the horizon, the beautiful dawn would soon let her be seen behind the golden curtain; a bugle call to the attention was the agreed signal, and we soon heard that terrible bugle call of death, which stirred our hearts, altered our expressions, and aroused us suddenly from our painful meditations. Worn out by fatigue and lack of sleep, I had just closed my eyes to nap when my ears were pieced by this fatal note. A trumpeter of the sappers (Jose Maria Gonzales) was the one who inspired us to scorn life and to welcome death. Seconds later the horror of this sound fled from among us, honour and glory replaced it. The columns advanced with as much speed as possible; shortly after beginning the march they were ordered to open fire while they were still out of range, but there were some officers who wisely disregarded the signal.

Alerted to our attack by the given signal, which all columns answered, the enemy vigorously returned our fire, which had not even touched him but had retarded our advance. Travis, to compensate for the small number of the defenders, had placed three or four rifles by the side of each man, so that the initial fire was very rapid and deadly. Our columns left along their path a wide trail of blood, of wounded and of dead. The bands from all the corps, gathered around our commander, sounded the charge; with a most vivid ardour and enthusiasm we answered that call which electrifies the heart, elevates the soul, and makes others tremble.

At 3:00am General Cos and his unit reached a point to the north-west corner of the defences, and ordered his men to lie flat on the ground about three hundred paces from the Alamo; they being composed of the Aldama *cazadores* and fusiliers, and one hundred fusiliers of the reserve militia of San Luis. They remained flat on the ground until five, when they received the signal to attack.

This was the *Degüello* bugle call. *Degüello* is a Spanish noun from the verb *degollar*, to describe the action of throat cutting, or more figuratively to describe that no quarter will be given, and complete destruction of the enemy with no mercy is intended.

An unidentified Mexican soldier in Cos's units left the following account concerning this part of the action. The soldier seems to have got his compass points wrong, thinking that south was north. It appears in Cheriton's *100 Days in Texas – The Alamo Letters*:

> I marched under the immediate command of General Cos and tell you what I saw. After a long wait we took our places at 3 o'clock am on the south side, a distance of 300 feet from the fort of the enemy. Here we remained flat on our stomachs until 5:30 (Whew! it was cold) when the signal to march was given by the President from the battery between the north and east. Immediately, General Cos cried 'Forward' and placing himself at the head of the attack, we ran to the assault, carrying scaling ladders, picks and spikes. Although the distance was short the fire from the enemy's cannon was fearful; we fell back; more than forty men fell around me in a few moments.

Sergeant Loranca recorded: 'The assault took place at 3:30am, on the 6th, and was so sudden that the fort had only time to discharge four of the eighteen cannon which it had. The fort Alamo had only one entrance, which was on the south, and the approach was made winding to impede the entrance of the cavalry. The Mexican infantry, with ladders, were lying down at musket-shot distance, awaiting the signal of assault, which was to be given from a fort about a cannon-shot to the east of the Alamo, where the President Santa Anna was with the music of the regiment of Dolores and his staff to direct the movements. In the act of assault confusion occurred, occasioned by darkness, in which the Mexican troops opened fire on each other. A culverin, a 16-pound howitzer, fired from the fort, swept off a whole company of the Battalion Almada, which made the attack on the point toward San Antonio.'

When the bugle call rang out, many Alamo defenders were asleep in their quarters or at their posts, apparently including the sentries, who were believed to be the first defenders to die that day. However, a captain, possibly William Blazeby, saw the Mexican advance as their units moved forward in the dim light and raised the alarm.

Colonel Travis had been resting in his room with his servant, Joe, who heard the alarm. Travis sprang up and seized his weapons, calling to Joe to follow him. As he ran across the compound he called out: 'Come on, boys, the Mexicans are upon us, and we'll give them Hell!' He took his post manning the big gun to the north-west, where the Mexicans were advancing in great numbers towards that area of the ramparts.

Captain Almaron Dickinson rushed into the side room of the chapel where his wife, Susanna, and their child Angelina were, and exclaimed: 'Great God, Sue, the Mexicans are inside our walls! All is lost! If they spare you, save my child.' With a parting kiss he drew his sword and with the noise of the terrible struggle for survival raging in different portions of the fortifications ringing in his ears, he went back up the slope to man the gun he had placed at the eastern end of the chapel.

Doctor Sutherland remembered: 'Captain Dickinson commanded a gun which bore from the small window in the east end of the church. It was in the second storey and there being no floor overhead, he erected a scaffold for the gun to stand upon. It was in the church that he fell.'

A cannonade from Travis's guns smashed through the Mexican ranks and left many of General Cos's men scattered across the ground. The Mexicans fell back, and a second cannonade caused them to falter. Having lost many men by the sustained firing of Travis's battery, and being annoyed by the firing of the Toluca Battalion, which sometimes went astray and among them from further north-east, General Cos ordered his men to veer right, so the north-west corner of the defences would at least protect them from this 'friendly fire'. Although this was a strong point of the defences, which they knew as Fortin de Condelle, they commenced their efforts to position their ladders and try to climb up to the top of the walls.

Colonel de la Pena recorded: 'It could be observed that a single cannon volley did away with half the company of chasseurs from Toluca, which was advancing a few paces from the column; Captain Jose Maria Herrera, who commanded it, died a few moments later; and Lieutenant Vences was also wounded. Another volley left many gaps among the ranks at the head, one of them being Colonel Duque, who was wounded in the thigh; Don Jose Maria Macotela, captain from Toluca, was seriously wounded and died shortly after.'

However, the Mexicans rallied and returned a terrible fire, which had an unnerving effect on the Alamo defenders, and Colonel Travis had just discharged his gun when a bullet hit him in the forehead. He fell down on the sloping firing ramp behind his gun; never to rise again.

Colonel de la Pena continued: 'Travis was seen to hesitate, but not about the death he would choose. He would take a few steps and stop, turning his proud face toward us to discharge his shots: he fought like a true soldier. Finally he died, but he died after trading his life very dearly. None of his men died with greater heroism, and they all died. Travis behaved like a hero; one must do him justice.'

Travis's slave, Joe, was recorded as saying: 'As Travis sat wounded on the ground General Mora, who was passing him, made a blow at him with his sword, which Travis struck up, and ran his assailant through the body, and both died on the same spot. This was poor Travis's last effort.'

The attackers began to reach the tops of the walls and surged over the ramparts at every vantage point. Eventually the defenders fell back to the sandbag ramparts and trenches at the barrack rooms and the mission church to the south-west. Fierce man-to-man fighting ensued and many Mexican soldiers were killed as they pursued them.

Mrs Dickinson recalled from inside the fort, 'Under the cover of darkness they approached the fortifications, and planting their scaling ladders against our walls just as light was approaching, they climbed up to the tops of walls and jumped down within, many of them to their immediate death – as fast as the front ranks were slain, they were filled up again with fresh troops.'

The furious Mexican soldiers had been ordered to kill all the defenders, including women and children, and the Texans expected no mercy. The hand-to-hand combat was fought in near darkness and in smoke-filled rooms and in this uncontrollable disorder many Mexican soldiers were slain by their own men. One can only imagine the bloody carnage and butchery that took place.

Captain Potter recorded:

This all passed within a few minutes after the bugle sounded. The garrison, when driven from the thinly manned outer defences, whose early loss was inevitable, took refuge in the buildings before described, but mainly in the long barrack; and it was not till then, when they became more concentrated and covered within, that the main struggle began. They were more concentrated as to space, not as to unity of command; for there was no communicating between buildings, nor, in all cases, between rooms. There was little need of command, however, to men who had no choice left but to fall where they stood before the weight of numbers. There was now no retreating from point to point, and each group of defenders had to fight and die in the den where it was brought to bay. From the doors, windows, and loopholes of the several rooms around the area the crack of the rifle and the hiss of the bullet came fierce and fast, as fast the enemy fell and recoiled in his first efforts to charge.

The gun beside which Travis fell was now turned against the buildings, as were also some others, and shot after shot was sent crashing through the doors and barricades of the several rooms. Each ball was followed by a storm of musketry and a charge; and thus room after room was carried at the point of the bayonet, when all within them died fighting to the last.

The struggle was made up of a number of separate and desperate combats, often hand to hand, between squads of the garrison and bodies of the enemy. The bloodiest spot about the fort was the long barrack and the ground in front of it, where the enemy fell in heaps.

Before the action reached this stage, the turning of Travis's gun by the assailants was briefly imitated by a group of the defenders. 'A small piece on a high platform', as it was described to me by General Bradburn, was wheeled by those who manned it against the large area after the enemy entered it. Some of the Mexican officers thought it did more execution than any gun which fired outward; but after two effective discharges it was silenced, when the last of its cannoneers fell under a shower of bullets. I cannot locate this gun with certainty, but it was probably the twelve-pound cannon which fired over the center of the west wall from a high commanding position. The smallness assigned to it perhaps referred only to its length.

Sergeant Felix Nunez was with Castrillon's men, and remembered, 'By this time the front door was battered down and the conflict had become general. The entire army came pouring in from all sides, and never in all my life did I witness or hear of such a hand-to-hand conflict. The Americans fought with the bravery and desperation of tigers, although seeing that they were contending against the fearful odds of at least two hundred-to-one, not one single one of them tried to escape or asked for quarter, the last one fighting with as much bravery and animation as the first. None of them hid in rooms nor asked for quarter, for they knew none would be given. On the contrary they all died like heroes, selling their lives as dear as possible.'

Joe stated: 'The handful of Americans retreated to such covers as they had and continued the battle until only one was left; a little, weakly man named Warner, who asked for quarter. He was spared by the soldiery, but on being conducted to Santa Anna he ordered him to be shot, and it was done.'

Colonel de la Pena stated: 'Our brave officers left nothing to be desired in the hour of trial, and if anyone failed in his duty, if anyone tarnished his honour, it was so insignificant that his shortcomings remained in the confusion of obscurity and disdain. Numerous feats of valour were seen in which many fought hand-to-hand; there were also some cruelties observed.'

It is likely that General Cos was aware that it was the battery of cannon under Colonel Travis that had caused dreadful casualties among his columns of troops, and the *Louisiana Advertiser* reported:

General Cos, on entering the fort, ordered Colonel Travis's servant to point out to him the body of his master. He did so, then Cos drew his sword and mangled his face and limbs with the malignant feelings of a savage.

Jim Bowie remained in his bed during the fighting, from where he could hear the noise of the battle. The rattle of small arms and the shouts and curses of the combatants got so close that he could hear the thuds and smashes as they struck each other with rifle butts and anything they could get their hands on. The Mexicans burst in and he brought two of them down with pistols before they shot him in the head and ran him through with their sabres and mutilated his body.

Another account states that Bowie was lying on the ground with his head in the lap of a Mexican woman known as Madame Andrea Candelaria, who had nursed him during his illness. The Mexican soldiers impaled him with their bayonets and tossed his body about like a plaything. His faithful nurse was cut across her chin during the incident.

Sergeant Loranca noted: 'After that we entered the Alamo, and the first thing we saw on entering a room at the right was the corpses of Bowie and Travis. Then we passed to the corridor which served the Texans as quarters, and here found all refugees which were left. President Santa Anna immediately ordered that they should be shot, which was accordingly done, excepting only a Negro and a woman having a little boy about a year old. She was said to be Travis's cook.'

Having spoken to Mrs Dickinson and Joe about Bowie's situation, Doctor Sutherland noted: 'As soon as the bodies of Travis and Bowie were shown by this man, they were brutally mutilated by the sword and bayonet. Colonel Bowie, being yet sick, was confined to his room, indicated on the diagram, which he had occupied from the beginning of the siege. It was there while suffering the tortures of disease, unable to lift his head from his pillow, that he was butchered. He was shot several times through the head, his brains spattering upon the wall near his bed-side.

On Colonel Bowie's body being brought out General Cos said that he was too brave a man to be burned like a dog; then added – 'never mind, throw him in.' It may be that he saw how mutilated the body was and he thought it better to destroy it rather than it be buried and possibly exhumed at a later date. This may be the case with many of the defenders.

Dr Sutherland remembered later: 'I had some curiosity to see the place, and when in Bexar nearly two years after the fall, I visited the room which Colonel Bowie had occupied and in which he was killed, when upon examination, I found the stain of his brains yet upon the wall precisely as it had been represented to me by the persons mentioned [Mrs Dickinson and Joe]. The stain remained upon the walls of the room until they were re-plastered. I frequently visited the place and pointed out the spot to others.'

The troops under the command of Colonels Morales and Minon began to charge forward towards the main entrance and the palisade in front of the chapel door, where Davy Crockett and his 'Tennessee Boys' were firing their muskets as fast as they could. The Mexicans noticed the accuracy of their marksmanship; and Crockett in particular because of his peculiar dress. Although suffering casualties, the Mexicans eventually reached the barricades and struggled to get beyond them.

As they did so, Colonel Castrillon and the Mexican soldiers who had fought their way southward through the long barracks joined the attack on Crockett and his men, and most of the surviving Texans were forced to the area to the south-east of the defences in front of the chapel doors, where they continued to put up a stubborn resistance.

This account by Sergeant Nunez concerning the death of Davy Crockett is at odds with that of Colonel de la Pena and some other Mexican troops:

> To recount the individual deeds of valor of the brave men who were slain in the Alamo would fill a volume as large as the History of Texas, nevertheless, there was one who perished in that memorable conflict who is entitled to a passing notice. The one to whom I refer was killed just inside of the front door. The peculiarity of his dress, and his undaunted courage attracted the attention of several of us, both officers and men.
>
> He was a tall American of rather dark complexion and had a long cuera (buck skin coat) and a round cap without any bill, and made of fox skin, with the long tail hanging down his back. This man apparently had a charmed life. Of the many soldiers who took deliberate aim at him and fired, not one ever hit him. On the contrary he never missed a shot.
>
> He killed at least eight of our men, besides wounding several others. This fact was observed by a lieutenant who had come in over the wall. He sprung at him and dealt him a deadly blow with his sword, just above the right eye, which felled him to the ground and in an instant he was pierced by not less than twenty bayonets. This lieutenant said that if all Americans had as many of our men as this one had, our army would have been annihilated before the Alamo could have been taken. He was about the last man that was killed.

The defenders now faced a three-pronged attack and were being pushed back. It would seem that their resistance broke at this point and a few retreated inside the church, while many scrambled out of the defences near the chapel and tried to make their escape towards the east and south-east.

Sergeant Loranca recorded, 'Sixty-two Texans who sallied from the east side of the fort, were received by the Lancers and all killed. Only one of these made resistance, a very active man, armed with a double-barrel gun and a single barrel pistol, with which he killed a corporal of the Lancers named Eugenio. These were all killed by the lance, except one, who ensconced himself under a bush and it was necessary to shoot him.'

The Mexicans broke through the door of the chapel, and as he fell back Robert Evans, realising his life was about to end, decided to try to ignite the stack of gunpowder that remained in the side room to the left of the main door, and to try to take as many of the enemy with him as he could. He lit a torch, but as he ran towards the kegs of powder the flames attracted the attention of the Mexican soldiers, and he was within striking distance when an officer realised his intentions and shot him down before he was able to complete the task.

Some Mexican combatants left reports that these men had died in less dignified situations, but they had been partly responsible for the deaths of hundreds of their countrymen, and their accounts would have been clouded by bitter resentment.

Alamo non-combatants suffered casualties among their small number. Anthony Wolf asked the Mexicans to show mercy to him and his sons, but they were killed in a room in full view of several survivors, and their bodies unceremoniously removed on bayonets. Joe remembered a black woman being killed while she was attempting to cross the Alamo compound during the battle, and her body was found lying between two cannon. Enrique Esparza stated that a young American boy, no older than he (8 to 9 years) was killed right beside him, while the boy was drawing a blanket around his shoulders. Colonel de la Pena recorded: '… several women were found inside and were rescued by Colonels Morales and Minon'.

Brigido Guerrero, who had changed allegiance from service with the Mexican Army under Colonel Domingo de Ugartechea to join the Texans, and who had assisted James Bowie in obtaining cattle for the Bexar garrison, was captured by the Mexicans and his life was in danger until he managed to convince them that he was a prisoner of the Texans and he was allowed to go free.

Enrique Esparza recorded: 'No tongue can describe the terror and horror of that last fight! The women and children were paralyzed with terror and faint from hunger when the Mexican soldiers rushed in after the fall of the Alamo. A poor paralytic, unable to speak – to tell them he was not a belligerent, was murdered before their eyes, as also a young fellow who had been captured some time previously and confined in the Alamo. Brigido Guerrero, a youth, was saved, as he managed to say he was not a Texan, but a Texan prisoner.'

Sergeant Nunez recorded: 'On the floor of the main building there was a sight which beggared all description. The earthen floor was nearly shoe-mouth deep in blood and weltering therein laid 500 dead bodies, many of them still clinched together with one hand, while the other held fast a sword, a pistol or a gun, which betokened the kind of conflict which had just ended.'

Mrs Dickinson stated that, 'Soon after he [her husband] left me, three unarmed gunners, who had abandoned their then useless guns came into the church where I was, and were shot down by my side.' One of them is believed to have been Jacob Walker, and she continued, 'I saw four Mexicans toss him in the air with their bayonets, and then shoot him. At this moment a Mexican officer came into the room and asked: 'Are you Mrs Dickinson? If you wish to save your life, follow me,' which she did, and although she was shot at and wounded, she was spared.

Enrique Esparza remembered: '… and the other Mexicans who escaped the butchery of Santa Anna's hordes were concealed in two storerooms in the courtyard of the Alamo proper in front of what is left of the old building, and that these rooms were on each side of the main entrance gate which led into the court from the outside.'

He also stated:

She [Madam Candelaria] was not there [in the Alamo]. She had been in it frequently before it fell, he says, and was there immediately afterwards, but was not present when the actual fall of the Alamo and the massacre of its patriotic defenders occurred.

A Mexican officer [probably Morales or Minon] related to some of the refugees, arrived just in time to save the women and children – but they were subjected to terrible usage and horrible abuse. Finally, someone obtained safe conduct for them at about two o'clock on the morning of the seventh to the house of Governor Musquiz on Main Plaza. Here the famished prisoners were served with coffee by the Musquiz domestics.

At daylight they were required to go before Santa Anna and take the oath of allegiance. Each mother was then given a blanket and two dollars by Santa Anna in person. The only two who escaped this additional humiliation were the two daughters of Navarro, who were spirited away from Musquiz' house by their father [uncle] – Jose Antonio Navarro. The body of Esparza's father, who was butchered with other Texans, was obtained by his brother, who was in the Mexican army, and was buried in the San Fernando Campo Santa, and thus he has the distinction of being the only Texan who escaped the funeral pyre.

Colonel de la Pena lamented:

This scene of extermination went on for an hour before the curtain of death covered and ended it. Shortly after six in the morning it was all finished. The Corps were beginning to reassemble and to identify themselves, their sorrowful countenances revealing the losses in the thinned ranks of their officers and comrades; when the commander-in-chief appeared. Santa Anna could see for himself the desolation among his battalions and that devastated area littered with corpses, with scattered limbs and bullets, with weapons and torn uniforms. Some of these were burning together with the corpses, which produced an unbearable and nauseating odour.

The bodies, with their blackened and bloody faces disfigured by a desperate death, their hair and uniforms burning at once, presented a dreadful and truly hellish sight. What trophies – those of the battlefield! Quite soon some of the bodies were left naked by the fire; others had been stripped naked by a disgraceful rapacity among our men. The enemy could be identified by their whiteness, by their robust and bulky shapes. What a sad spectacle, that of the dead and dying! What a horror, to inspect the area and find the remains of friends – ! With what anxiety did some seek others, and with what ecstasy did they embrace one another! Questions followed one after the other, even while the bullets were still whistling around, in the midst of the groans of the wounded and the last breaths of the dying.

According to the *Louisiana Advertiser* of 28 March 1836: 'The Texians fought desperately until daylight, when seven only of the garrison were found alive; we regret to say that Colonel David Crockett and his companion Mr [Jesse] Benton, also the gallant Colonel Bonham of S C were of the number who cried for quarter, but were told there was no mercy for them. They then continued fighting until the whole were butchered.'

The number of men said to have survived the initial fighting varies, but Ramon Martinez Caro was Santa Anna's secretary, and in his account he stated: 'The enemy died to a man and its loss may be said to have been 183 men, the sum total of their force. Six women who were captured were set at liberty. Among the 183 killed there were five who were discovered by General Castrillón hiding after the assault. He took them immediately to the presence of His Excellency [Santa Anna] who had come up by this time. When he presented the prisoners, he was severely reprimanded for not having killed them on the spot, after which he turned his back upon Castrillón while the soldiers stepped out of their ranks and set upon the prisoners until they were all killed.'

Colonel de la Pena recorded:

> Some seven men had survived the general carnage, and under the protection of General Castrillon, they were brought before Santa Anna. Among them was one of great stature, well-proportioned, with regular features, in whose face there was the imprint of adversity but in whom one also noticed a degree of resignation and nobility that did him honour. He was the naturalist David Crockett ... Santa Anna answered Castrillon's intervention on Crockett's behalf with a gesture of indignation and addressing himself to the sappers, the troops closest to him, ordered his execution.
>
> The commanders and officers were outraged at this action and did not support the order, hoping that once the fury of the moment had blown over, these men would be spared; but several officers who were around the president and who, perhaps, had not been present during the moment of danger became noteworthy by an infamous deed, surpassing the soldiers in cruelty. They thrust themselves forward, in order to flatter their commander, and with swords in hand fell upon these unfortunate, defenceless men just as a tiger leaps upon his prey. Though tortured before they were killed, these unfortunates died without complaining and without humiliating themselves before their torturers.
>
> It was rumoured that General Sesma was one of them; I will not bear witness to this, for though present I turned away horrified in order not to witness such a barbarous scene ... I confess that the very memory of it makes me tremble, and that my ear can still hear the penetrating, doleful sound of the victims.

It was recorded that General Castrillon rushed from the scene, apparently horror-struck, sought his quarters, and did not leave them for several days; and he hardly spoke to Santa Anna after.

Susanna Dickinson remembered:

> As we passed through the enclosed ground in front of the church, I saw heaps of dead and dying ... I recognized Colonel Crockett lying dead and mutilated between the church and the two-storey barrack building, and even remember seeing his peculiar cap lying by his side.
>
> Santa Anna ordered that all the American bodies were to be dragged out of the Alamo and burned. However, the uniforms were so bedraggled and stained, and the faces of the dead combatants so besmeared with blood and blackened with dirt, that it was difficult to distinguish

110

between them. Santa Anna instructed that their faces be cleaned to identify them, and ordered that none of his men were to be burned with the Americans. He stood for a moment gazing at the horrid and ghastly spectacle before him, but soon retired and was seen no more.

The Mexicans brought wood from a nearby forest and that same evening they lit a bonfire. This was no dignified funeral pyre, as the remains of the Alamo defenders were unceremoniously thrown onto it and disposed of. Their own comrades received more dignified treatment as most of them were buried in the city.

Francisco Antonio Ruiz, the Alcalde of San Antonio, stated:

> He [Santa Anna] directed me to call upon some of the neighbours to come with carts to carry the dead to the cemetery; and also to accompany him, as he was desirous to have Colonels Travis, Bowie and Crockett shown to him ... After the Mexicans were taken out, he ordered wood to be brought to burn the bodies of the Texans. He sent a company of dragoons with me to bring wood and dry branches from the neighbouring forests. About 3 o'clock in the afternoon of the next day they commenced laying wood and dry branches upon which a file of dead bodies were placed, more wood was piled on them and another file brought, and in this manner all were arranged in layers. Kindling wood was distributed through the pile and at 8 o'clock it was lighted. The dead Mexicans of Santa Anna's army were taken to the graveyard, but not having sufficient room for them, I ordered some of them to be thrown in the river, which was done on the same day. The men burned numbered 182. I was with some of the neighbours collecting the dead bodies and placing them on the funeral pyre.

Sergeant Loranca stated: 'There in front of the fosse [trench] were gathered the bodies of all those who died by the lance, and those killed in the fort, making a total of 283 persons, including a Mexican found among them, who, it appears, had come from La Bahia (Goliad) with dispatches; and here they were ordered to be burned, there being no room in the Campo Santo or burying ground, it being all taken with the bodies of upwards of four hundred Mexicans, who were killed in the assault.'

A citizen of Bexar County named Candelario Villanueva, who had been a member of Captain Seguin's company in 1835 and 1836, made a sworn statement on 26 August 1859, in which he stated: 'After the fall of the Alamo I went there and among the dead bodies of those lying inside the rooms I recognized the body of Gregorio Esparza; I also saw the bodies of Antonio Fuentes; Toribio Losoyo; Guadalupe Rodriguez and other Mexicans who had fallen in the defence of the Alamo, and also the bodies of Colonels Travis, Bowie and Crockett, and other

Americans I had previously known. I saw Francisco Esparza and his brothers take the body of Gregorio Esparza and carry it off towards the Campo Santo for internment; the bodies of the Americans were laid in a pile and burnt.'

A historic memorial plaque that was erected on 6 March 2004 by the Alamo Defenders Descendants Association in what is stated to be the 20-acre plot where some Alamo defenders were buried, repeats the words of an article published in the *San Antonio Daily Express* for 6 July 1906: 'August Beisenbach, city clerk of San Antonio, states that when he was an 8 year old boy playing on the Alameda (Commerce Street) he witnessed the exhuming of bodies or remains consisting of bones and fragments of bones, of victims of the siege of the Alamo that had been interred near the place where the bodies had been burned and originally buried, and saw their transfers to the old cemetery on Powder House Hill (Oddfellows Cemetery), this, he states, happened in 1856. The fragments of the bodies had been first buried in 1836 and some in 1837. Mr Beisenbach states that these bodies are buried midway between the monuments of Captain R A Gillespie and Captain Samuel H Walker.' The cemetery is situated at Paso Hondo Street, south-east of the Alamo.

It is thought that Santa Anna had the bodies of the defenders burned to prevent them from gaining martyrdom status. However, Santa Anna is known to have been shown the bodies of Travis, Crockett and Bowie, who were all reported to have been badly mutilated, and many of the defenders had been stripped and their bodies treated badly, so it is more likely that he realised that if they had been buried they could have been exhumed and the evidence exposed, so he decided to destroy them all. It has to be considered that the Mexican army were only at the start of the campaign, and it is known that Santa Anna desired a swift victory. He had already shown his frustration at how the siege had delayed his plans, so would he have been so concerned about martyrdom and memorials? Surely if he did have such a train of thought he would also have taken the time to have his men destroy the chapel to prevent it from being the memorial it did eventually become.

Mr Ruiz concluded: 'The gallantry of the few Texans who defended the Alamo was really wondered at by the Mexican army. Even the generals were astonished at their vigorous resistance, and how dearly the victory had been bought.' Santa Anna dictated an announcement of a glorious victory, and his aide, Colonel Juan Almonte, privately noted: 'One more such glorious victory and we are finished.'

Santa Anna wrote to General Tornel: 'The bearer takes with him one of the flags of the enemy's battalion captured today.' He is believed to have been referring to the flag that the Greys flew at the Alamo, which was captured by Mexican forces after the battle. It has survived the years, and is in the Museum of the Insurrection in Churubusco, Mexico City. A replica hangs in an alcove inside the Alamo Chapel.

José Juan Sánchez-Navarro stated:

> Long live our country, the Alamo is ours! Today at five in the morning, the assault was made by four columns under the command of General Cos and Colonels Duque, Romero, and Morales. His Excellency the President commanded the reserves. The firing lasted half an hour. Our *jefes*, officers, and troops, at the same time as if by magic, reached the top of the wall, jumped within, and continued fighting with side arms. By six thirty there was not an enemy left. I saw actions of heroic valor I envied. I was horrified by some cruelties, among others, the death of an old man named Cochran and of a boy about fourteen. The women and children were saved. Travis, the commandant of the Alamo died like a hero; but the braggart son-in-law of Veramendi [died] like a coward. The troops were permitted to pillage. The enemy have suffered a heavy loss: twenty-one field pieces of different calibre, many arms and munitions. Two hundred fifty-seven of their men were killed: I have seen and counted their bodies. But I cannot be glad because we lost eleven officers with nineteen wounded, including the valiant Duque and González; and two hundred forty-seven of our troops were wounded and one hundred ten killed. It can truly be said that with another such victory as this we'll go to the devil.

Twelve non-combatants are known to have been allowed to survive the battle of the Alamo. Alijo Pérez Junior was just seventeen days short of his first birthday on the day of the battle, and was the last-known survivor. His father was Alejo Pérez, and he was with his mother, Juana Navarro Alsbury, and stepfather, Horace Arlington Alsbury at the Alamo. He was employed as a policeman in San Antonio, where he married Antonia Rodríguez in 1853, and they had four children. He died on 19 October 1918, aged 93. Doctor Sutherland recorded: 'It was said that no less than thirty-three widows were left in the town of Gonzales and vicinity, in a manner destitute.'

The *North Melbourne Gazette* for 11 August 1899, and various other Australian newspapers during the course of the year, published 'The Fall of the Alamo', an article that had first appeared in the popular magazine *Texas Siftings*. The editor who wrote the piece was Alexander Edwin Sweet (1841–1901), a Canadian-born journalist who lived in San Antonio from 1849 to 1858. The magazine was first published in Austin in 1881, by Sweet and Belfast-born John Armoy Knox (1851–1906), and a London office was opened in 1887, the year of Queen Victoria's golden jubilee:

The massacre of a band of Texans at the Alamo by an overwhelming Mexican army under General Santa Anna on 6th of March 1835, after a siege of eleven days, is the most important event in the history of Texas.

The refusal of the Texans to surrender, and their successful effort to hold their foes at bay, enabled General Houston to concentrate his forces. Moreover, the slaughter of the heroes of the Alamo transformed their brethren in arms from men into demons, and when the day of reckoning came, a few weeks after at San Jacinto, they attacked the Mexicans with a fiendish ferocity that was absolutely irresistible. With 'Remember the Alamo' for their battle cry, they slaughtered the terrified Mexicans like sheep, actually killing more of their number and capturing the rest of the Mexican army along with General Santa Anna himself, thereby securing the independence of Texas. Had it not been for the massacre at the Alamo the probabilities are that the Texas Revolution would have been crushed.

In February 1836, a portion of Santa Anna's army unexpectedly appeared on the outskirts of the town of San Antonio. The Texas garrison, consisting of 150 men under Colonel Travis, were taken by surprise, but succeeded in retreating into the Alamo on the east side of the river. Fort Alamo consisted of a large enclosure of five acres surrounded by 2 stockades and high walls of masonry. The fort included a chapel and a convent, massively constructed stone buildings, and was defended by eight pieces of heavy artillery. While the walls were well adapted to keeping out Indians they were too weak to resist artillery. The story of the Alamo has been told so often that we will not attempt to reproduce it in detail. After eleven days of unceasing bombardment, General Santa Anna made his arrangements to take the Alamo by storm, the Texans rejecting every overture to surrender.

Sunday, 6th March, was the fatal day. Shortly after midnight the Mexican began its march to assigned positions. At 4 o'clock the bugle call sounded, and Santa Anna headed an advance. Grape, musket, and rifle balls hit them, and twice they were repelled; combined, forming a dense mass, at last, reaching the tops of some houses forming the wall of the fort affected an entrance to the enclosed yard. About the same time they forced a breach in the wall and captured one of the Texan guns. This was at once turned upon the convent, to which the Americans had retreated. The cannonade of the besieged still did fearful execution, but the feeble garrison could not resist overwhelming numbers. The surviving Texans retreated to the chapel, and there took place the most desperate hand-to-hand fight that ever occurred. The Texans fought to the last gasp, and when all was over the chapel was a slaughter-house, clogged with hundreds of mangled corpses.

The boyhood of the editor of 'Texas Siftings' was spent almost within shadow of the old Alamo, and I heard many interesting stories of the memorable events from the lips of old Texans, who knew whereof they spoke. Travis, the heroic leader of the Texans, was killed early in the fight, cheering his men. The body of the immortal David Crockett was found in the baptistry of the chapel, the door of which was congested with second-hand Mexicans.

Referring to Crockett, an interesting story is told by an old Mexican who was in Santa Anna's army, and in one of the attacking columns. When the Mexican regiment got within gunshot range of the fort a tall man wearing a cap appeared on the roof of the chapel. He shot the Mexican colonel off his horse and disappeared. This man was undoubtedly David Crockett, for he was the only Texan wearing a cap. He wore a coon-skin cap.

Colonel Bowie, of Bowie-knife fame, was in a dying condition from typhoid fever at the time of the battle. He was probably the last man killed. He was lying on the ground with his head in the lap of a Mexican woman who nursed him during his illness. The Mexican soldiers impaled him with their bayonets and tossed his body about like a plaything. His faithful nurse, Madame Candelaria [Andrea Castanon Villaneuva, 1803– 99], is still living in San Antonio, and bears in her face the marks of a wound made at that time by the bayonet of one of Bowie's murderers [on her chin].

General Santa Anna and other high Mexican officers had a special spite at Bowie. He had married Ursula Veramendi, the daughter of Governor Veramendi. The Mexicans thought because he had married into an aristocratic Mexican family he should have sided with them instead of with his own countrymen.

An old Mexican, who as a boy visited the Alamo on the day after the massacre, was an eye-witness of the disposition made of the bodies of the slaughtered Texans. A number of bodies were placed side by side on the ground and covered with fence rails. Then another layer of corpses was placed on the fence rails and covered with brush and set on fire. The bodies of all the Texans were thus burned, and the narrator said with uplifted eyes and hands that it was muy feo, which means very ugly.

There are conflicting accounts of the number of Mexicans engaged in the battle, but 2500 is a conservative estimate. Of these probably not less than 800 were killed and wounded. The extraordinary number of Mexicans killed in all the engagements of the Texas revolution is explained by the fact that the Texans were mostly from Kentucky and Tennessee; men who could bark squirrels with a rifle all day long. Such marksmen rarely missed as large a target as a Mexican. In fact, almost all the Mexicans killed in these fights were shot through the head.

The writer remembers seeing in the old Campo Santo, of San Antonio, a pile of skulls, each one of which was bored by a rifle ball. These were the skulls of Mexicans who fell in what was known as 'The Grass Fight' near that town. The Mexicans laboured under the double disadvantage of being poor shots and being armed with old-fashioned escopetan, or blunderbusses. Much better troops suffered similar disaster at New Orleans at the hands of the same type of American soldiers.

When the Alamo fell, San Antonio was a small Mexican village. Now it is a progressive American city of 50,000 inhabitants, with water works, electric lights, rapid transit schools, churches, and all the other requirements of the highest order of modern civilisation.

When Susanna Dickinson, who came to be known as 'The Lady of the Alamo', was released from Bexar by Santa Anna on the day after the fall of the Alamo and sent to Gonzales, he sent with her a letter meant for the people of that town, which gives an interesting insight into his attitude towards the Texans at that time. It appeared in the *Fort Worth Press* for 14 March 1836:

The General-in-Chief of the Army of Operations of the Mexican Republic to the inhabitants of Texas citizens! The causes which have conducted to this frontier a part of the Mexican army are not unknown to you; a parcel of audacious adventurers, maliciously protected by some inhabitants of a neighbouring republic, dared to invade our territory, with the intention of dividing among themselves the fertile lands that are contained within the spacious Department of Texas; and even had the boldness to entertain the idea of reaching the capital of the Republic.

It became necessary to check and chastise such enormous daring, and in consequence, some exemplary punishments have already taken place in San Patricio, Lipantitian and this city.

I am pained to find amongst those adventurers the names of some colonists to whom had been granted repeated benefits, and had no motive of complaint against the government of their adopted country.

These ungrateful men must also necessarily suffer the just punishment that the laws and the public vengeance demand. But if we are bound to punish the criminal we are not the less compelled to protect the innocent. It is thus that the inhabitants of this country, let their origin be what it may, who should not appear to be implicated in such iniquitous rebellion, shall be respected in their persons and property, provided they come forward and report themselves to the commander of the troops within eight days after they should have arrived in their respective settlements in order to justify their conduct and to receive a document guaranteeing to them the right of enjoying that which lawfully belongs to them.

Bexarians! Return to your homes and dedicate yourselves to your domestic duties. Your city and the fortress of the Alamo are already in possession of the Mexican army, composed of your own fellow citizens, and rest assured that no mass of foreigners will ever interrupt your repose, and much less attack your lives and plunder your property. The supreme government has taken you under its protection and will seek for your good.

Inhabitants of Texas! I have related to you the orders that the Army of Operations I have the honour to command comes to execute, and therefore the good will have nothing to fear. Fulfil always your duties as Mexican citizens, and you may expect the protection and benefit of the laws; and rest assured that you will never have reason to repeat yourselves of having observed such conduct, for I pledge you in the name of the supreme authorities of the nation, and as your fellow citizen and friend, that what has been promised you will be faithfully performed.

Apparently, the letter was not enthusiastically received in Gonzales, and only a few days later Colonel Fannin's command at Goliad was executed, after surrendering, on the orders of Santa Anna – 'fellow citizen and friend'.

***

The first report on the fall of the Alamo was relayed to the outside world by two ranchers named Anselmo and Andrew Bergana, who reached Gonzales on 11 March, at about the same time as General Sam Houston and his staff arrived there direct from the Convention at Washington-on-the-Brazos.

News at that time travelled not so fast, and delays in the relay of information, which filtered south into Mexico and north through Texas and the United States, and then across the sea, meant that by the time some British readers heard about the fall of the Alamo, the defenders had been dead for nearly three months.

The first accounts of the battle of the Alamo and the Texas Revolution were reported in newspapers in Britain and around the world during September 1836. The original of this report appeared in the *Louisiana Advertiser* for 28 March 1836, and the *New Orleans True American* for 29 March 1836, and includes some interesting suggestions:

We learn by the passengers of the schooner *Comanche*, eight days from Texas, that on 25 February the Texian garrison in Bexar, of 150 men, commanded by Lieutenant Colonel William B Travis, was attacked by the advance division of General Santa Anna's army, consisting of 2,000 men, who were repulsed with the loss of many killed, between 500 and 800 men, without the loss of one man of the Texians.

About the same time Colonel Johnson, with a party of 70 men, while reconnoitring the westward of San Patricio, was surrounded in the night by a large body of Mexican troops. In the morning the demand, of surrender was made by the Mexican Commander, unconditionally, which was refused; but an offer of surrender was made as prisoners of war, which was exceeded to by the Mexicans; but no sooner had the

Texians marched out of their quarters and stacked their arms, than a general fire was opened upon them by the whole Mexican force. The Texians attempted to escape, but only three of them succeeded – one of whom was Colonel Johnson.

Between 25 February and 2 March, the Mexicans were employed in forming entrenchments around the Alamo and bombarding the place. On 2 March, Colonel Travis wrote that 200 shells had been thrown into the Alamo, without injuring a man. On 1 March the garrison of Alamo received a reinforcement of 32 Texians from Gonzales, having forced their way through the enemy's lines, making the number of Alamo 182 men.

On 6 March, about midnight, the Alamo was assaulted by the whole force of the Mexican army, commanded by Santa Anna in person; the battle was desperate until daylight, when only seven men belonging to the Texian garrison were found alive, who cried for quarter, but were told that there was no mercy for them; they continued fighting until the whole were butchered. One woman, Mrs Dickinson, and a Negro of Travis, were the only persons whose lives were spared. We regret to say that Colonel David Crockett, his companion Mr Benton, and Colonel Bonham, of South Carolina, were among the number slain. General Bowie was murdered in his bed, sick and helpless. General Cos, on entering the fort, ordered the servant of Colonel Travis to point out the body of his master. He did so, when Cos drew his sword and mangled the face and limbs with the malignant feeling of a Comanche savage. The bodies of the slain were thrown into a heap in the centre of the Alamo, and burned.

The loss of the Mexicans in storming the place was not less than 1,000 killed and mortally wounded, and as many wounded – making their loss in the first assault between 2,000 and 3,000 men. The flag used by the Mexicans was a blood red one, in place of a constitutional one.

Immediately after the capture General Santa Anna sent Mrs Dickinson and the servant to General Houston's camp, accompanied by a Mexican with a flag, who was bearer of a note from General Santa Anna, offering the Texians peace and a general amnesty if they would lay down their arms and submit to his government. General Houston's reply was, 'True, sir, you have succeeded in killing some of our brave men, but the Texians are not yet conquered.' The effect of the fall of Bexar throughout Texas was electrical. Every man who could use a rifle, and was in a condition to take the field, marched forthwith to the seat of war. It is believed that not less than 4,000 riflemen were on their way to the army when the Comanche sailed, determined to wreak their vengeance on the Mexicans.

General Houston had burnt Gonzales, and fallen back on the Colorado, with about 1000 men. Colonel Fanning was in the fort at Goliad, a very strong position, well supplied with munitions and provisions, with from 400 to 500 men. The general determination of the people of Texas is to abandon all their occupations and pursuits of peace, and continue in arms until every Mexican east of the Rio del Norte shall be exterminated.

Colonel Crockett was in the garrison of San Antonio, and Colonel Jessie Benton, it was also feared was in the engagement, and one of the victims.

On 4 May 1836, Dr J.H. Barnard visited the Alamo fort, and stated: 'As soon as the troops left town in the morning, a large fire streamed up from the Alamo, and, as soon as they had fairly left, Dr [Jack] Shackelford and myself, accompanied by Señor Reriz [Ruiz] and some other of the citizens walked over to see the state in which they [had] left it. We found the fire proceeding from a church, where a platform had been built extending from the great door to the top of the wall on the back side for the purpose of taking up artillery to the top of the church. This was made of wood, and was too far consumed for any attempt to be made to extinguish it. The walls of the church being built of solid masonry, of course would be little injured by the fire.'

Doctor Sutherland remembered: 'The room [where Bowie was killed] has since been demolished, together with the walls which Travis defended, and the barracks are all gone. The Vandal hand of progress has done its work. The old church alone, where Dickinson fell, remains, and the wandering tourist is pointed to this room or that within it, and told that here or there is where the noble Travis, or Bowie, or Crockett fell, when in truth they fell not in the church at all, but, as I have said on the ground outside, while the truck cart of traffic rumbles over the identical ground that drank in the life blood of those devoted men.'

10

'REMEMBER THE ALAMO!'

The siege stalled the Mexican Army's progress and allowed Sam Houston to gather troops and supplies. However, the Mexicans under General Jose de Urrea launched an offensive to retake the Texas Gulf Coast, gaining several victories over the Texans. The Texans were duped into surrendering at the battle of Coleto Creek on 20 March 1836, and over 400 prisoners, led by Colonel James Fannin, were held at Presidio La Bahia (Fort Defiance) in Goliad. On the morning of 27 March 1836, Palm Sunday, under the orders of Santa Anna, they were executed.

A memorial at La Bahia displays the words: 'Grave of J.W. Fannin and His Men. After battle of Coleto (March 19–20 1836), where a Texas army under Colonel James Walker Fannin met defeat by Mexicans in superior numbers, the Texas soldiers were held in Presidio La Bahia, supposedly as war prisoners. However, by order of Mexican General Antonio Lopez de Santa Anna, approximately 400 of Fannin's men were marched out and massacred on Palm Sunday, March 27, 1836. The wounded were shot one by one in the fort compound. Colonel Fannin was the last to die …'

The following particulars are from the *New York Advocate* of 18 May 1836:

We have been politely favoured with the following extract of a letter written to a gentleman of this city, from Nacogdoches, which goes still farther to corroborate the account received by the *Levant*, which we publish today.

The substance of which is, that an express has arrived here, via Nacogdoches, from Texas, and is confirmed by General Gaines, that General Houston, of Texas, has conquered Santa Anna and his army. Santa Anna and his soldiers are all prisoners. The forces of Santa

Anna were estimated at 1100, and those of Houston's army destroyed half of the Mexicans, and the loss on his side was six killed and twenty wounded.

Army Headquarters, April 1836 – To the People towards Nacogdoches: 'We met Santa Anna on the 21st [at San Jacinto]; we attacked him with 600 men; he had 1,100 infantry, two howitzers – we entirely routed his whole force, killed half of his men, and took the rest prisoners. Santa Anna and all his principal officers are our prisoners.

The saddle of Santa Anna was taken and brought in, and is of a costly order, being estimated as worth between 6 or 800 dollars, and the express who brought in the news, rode on the horse of Santa Anna.

All this is indeed cheering news, calculated to arouse all the better feelings, which are implanted in the hearts of those who can rejoice at the triumph of free men over their civil and savage oppressors. The intelligence received early yesterday morning, and which is also published, will be seen to be confirmed by the news brought by the Levant, with the difference only that the numbers of the enemy killed and taken by General Houston, vary in amount.

'The history of war does not furnish a parallel to the battle. We had 6 killed and 20 wounded. I have not time or I would send on a full report. I will do that in course of tomorrow. I again call on my fellow citizens to come to the field; let us fall on and conquer the remaining troops, and our country is free; turn out at once, there is no excuse now; let us do the work at once.' – Thomas Rush, Secretary at War.

'I certify the above to be a true copy of the express just received from the Secretary of War, who was himself in the battle.' – A Houston – to J. R. Dunn.

It would seem that the Bowie knife was used extensively during the battle of San Jacinto. William Tait, the editor of *Tait's Edinburgh Magazine* for May 1843, stated: 'I have heard that a blow from one, well wielded, is sufficient to break a man's arm. I myself have seen skulls of Mexicans brought from the battle ground of San Jacinto, on which Texas gained her independence, cleft nearly through the thickest part of the bone, behind evidently at one blow, and with sufficient force to throw out extensive cracks like those of a starred glass. This is more true to fact than complimentary to Mexican valour.'

***

After nearly ten years of remaining a republic, Texas became a part of the United States on 29 December 1845, and under the title 'United States and Texas', several newspapers in Britain and the Empire carried the following article towards the end of the year:

The *Acadia* brings news no less important than that the Congress of Texas has rejected the conditions for peace with Mexico signed by its own officer, and has passed resolutions agreeing to annexation with the United States. The question of annexation was introduced by President Jones to the Texan Legislature in a long speech on the 16th of June and on the 18th the Senate passed resolutions of annexation, and sent them to the House. The House laid them on the table, and, passing their own, sent them to the Senate on the 19th. A strife arose as to which body should have the honour of originating the successful resolutions, and finally the following, which originated with the Senate, were unanimously adopted in both branches:-

Whereas the Government of the United States hath proposed the following terms, guarantees, and conditions on which the people and territory of the republic of Texas may be erected into a new state, to be called the state of Texas, and admitted as one of the states of the American Union, to wit: [Here follow the resolutions of the United States Congress.] And whereas, by said terms, this consent or the existing Government of Texas is required, therefore: –

Section 1 – Be it enacted by the Senate and House of Representatives of the republic of Texas in Congress assembled that the Government of Texas doth consent that the people and territory of the republic of Texas may be erected into a new state, to be called the state of Texas, with a republican form of Government, to be adopted by the people of the said republic, by deputies in convention assembled, in order that the same may be admitted as one of the states of the American Union; and said consent is given on the terms, guarantees, and conditions set forth in the preamble to this joint resolution.

Section 2 – Be it further resolved, that the proclamation of the President of the Republic of' Texas, bearing date May 5th 1845, and the election of deputies to sit in convention at Austin on the 4th day of July next, for the adoption of a constitution for the state of Texas, and in accordance therewith, hereby receive the consent of the existing Government of Texas.

Section 3 – Be it further resolved that the President of Texas is hereby requested immediately to furnish the Government of the United States, through their accredited Minister near this Government, with a copy of this joint resolution; also to furnish the convention to assemble at Austin on the 4th of July next with a copy of the same and the same shall take effect from and after its passage.

The Treaty of Peace, which had been signed with Mexico, was considered by the Senate in secret session on the 21st of June, and rejected by a unanimous vote, and the injunction of secrecy removed. On the passage of the annexation resolution, an express was despatched by President Jones to the Commander of the United States' troops at Fort

Jessie, requesting that two regiments of the United States' troops should be sent to the frontier of Texas.

Simultaneous with the receipt of this requisition, General Taylor is said to have received orders from the War Department to put his troops in motion. Immediate preparations were made for a start, and the 3rd and 4th Regiments of Infantry embarked on board the steam-boats *Yazoo, Cote, Joyeuse, Rodolph* and *De Solo*, for Orleans; there, according to one account, to await the action of the Texan Convention, which met on the 4th instant at Austin, when they would move by water to Corpus Christi; or, as is more probable, thence to embark as soon as transports could be procured for the mouth of the Rio Grande. The 2nd Regiment of Mounted Dragoons, under the command of Colonel Twiggs, at the same time took up their line of march, to strike across to the Rio Grande through Texas.

The *Acadia* brings over Mr McLane, the new American minister, to facilitate the Oregon negotiation. President Polk's friends assert that amongst the measures he will recommend to the next Congress will be a reduction of the present high tariff. It is now so exorbitant that it assumes an anti-commercial character as regards other nations, while it forces up the prices of home fabrics so high that it imposes a tax on the people, which goes into the pockets of the manufacturers, although all must admit that a tolerably high tariff is necessary to protect and encourage the manufacturing interests of America.

Mr Walker, of the United States Cabinet, has written a letter to the Mississippi, in which he says 'At present my chief occupation is with the details of the tariff. It must be reduced to the revenue standard.'

Mr Bancroft, of the Cabinet, is known to be similarly employed, and the Washington Union (Government official), which speaks, as it were, with the voice of the Government, strongly enforces the view of Mr Walker.

A large company of settlers for California is assembling at St Louis, where public meetings have been held on the subject. Emigration of this character will settle the question in California. It will soon be the nucleus of a great Republic.

The Alamo church was purchased by the state of Texas in 1883 and was managed by the city of San Antonio. In 1905, the state purchased the rest of the mission property and turned the complex into a museum and shrine. In 1907 the Daughters of the Republic of Texas persuaded the legislature to buy the Alamo complex.

The 'Heroes of the Alamo' Monument was erected in the Texas State Capitol grounds at Austin in Texas in 1891. It is made from pink granite, and four columns at each corner bear the names of the defenders. The inscription on the north face reads: 'Thermopylae Had

Men Messengers of Defeat, the Alamo had none.' The east face reads: 'God and Texas, Victory or Death.' On the top stands a bronze statue of a Texan holding a muzzle-loading rifle.

In August 1913, British newspapers reported on the construction of an Alamo Memorial in San Antonio, but it was never built:

> The highest memorial monument in the World is to be erected at San Antonio, Texas, in honour of the soldiers who defended the Alamo in that city against the Mexicans during the war for independence of Texas.
>
> The tower will be 802 feet high, and will be the highest structure of any kind in the world with the exception of the Eiffel Tower in Paris. This structure will be a great deal more than a memorial monument, since it will contain four auditoriums, a museum, art gallery, statuary hall, and an individual exhibition room for each country in the State.
>
> The cost is estimated at £400,000. The base of the structure will be of solid granite, and 50 feet high. Surmounting the ledge at the top of this base will be statues of heroic size, of Travis, Crockett, Bowie, and Bonham, the four leaders of the Texans who were killed while defending the Alamo.
>
> Four elevators, one at each corner of the tower, will run to the 120 feet level, while one elevator placed in the centre of the tower will run from this point to the dome, where an observatory will be maintained by the Federal Government. A powerful searchlight is to be placed at the top of the tower. The monument is to be built by public subscriptions.

In early 1931 British newspapers reported on another project that did not come to fruition: 'The national shrine of St Anthony "New Alamo" costing one million dollars is planned for San Antonio, Texas. The shrine will commemorate three anniversaries – the 200th anniversary of the founding of San Antonio (City of St Anthony), which will be observed in March; the 700th anniversary of the death of St Anthony, which will be on 13 June, and. the centenary of the fall of the Alamo, 6 March 1936.'

A British newspaper for early 1927 reported under the title: 'The Bowie Knife':

> Among minor centenaries one should interest every boy who has ever read a 'Buffalo Bill' yarn, or grown-ups who delight in the Wild West dramas at 'the pictures' is the hundredth anniversary of the Bowie knife, which was 'invented' by Colonel Jim Bowie, of Texas, exactly a hundred years ago.
>
> Colonel Jim was such a hero as a great new Wild West film might be 'shot' around, and in 1826 (says an exchange), in a melee at Natchez, in

which six men were killed and 15 wounded, the redoubtable Bowie slew one of his antagonists with a weapon which we are told, was 'made out of a blacksmith's rasp or file.'

Colonel Bowie afterwards took this weapon to Philadelphia, and had it made into what afterwards became famous as the Bowie knife, a double-edged weapon 10 to 15 inches long, by 1 inch wide.

The gallant Colonel afterwards lost his own life in battle, fighting desperately in the great struggle of 'The Alamo' in the Texan War of 1836.

***

In 1838 Santa Anna led a makeshift army against French forces who had invaded his home territory of Vera Cruz, in what came to be known as the Pastry War. He was seriously wounded by grapeshot fired from a French cannon, and he had to have his leg amputated, which Santa Anna had buried in his Vera Cruz hacienda. When he assumed the Presidency again in 1842, he had the leg exhumed and, after parading it through Mexico City, he had it reburied beneath a monument in an elaborate state funeral that included cannon salvos, poetry and speeches. However, in 1844, when public opinion had turned against him yet again, rioters tore down the monument, dug up the leg, and dragged it through the streets of the capital shouting 'Death to the cripple!'

Santa Anna had a prosthetic cork and wooden leg made, and during the battle of Cerro Gordo near Xalapa in Vera Cruz, fought on 18 April 1847 during the Mexican–American War, the 4th Illinois Infantry surprised him in an ambush and he fled – leaving the leg behind, which the Americans seized as a war trophy and took it back to their home state. It was paraded at country fairs, and the showman P.T. Barnum claimed it for display in his museum, until it found its way into the Illinois State Military Museum in Springfield. The Mexican government and the State of Texas have both made repeated requests that the limb belongs with them but they have all been denied.

Santa Anna was known to chew the flavourless sap of the sapodilla tree, which had been long chewed by Mexico's Maya people. On 5 May 1951, several newspapers reported the following, under the title, By Gum! – It's Good:

About 1870 a Mexican General, Antonio Lopez de Santa Anna, Dictator and President of Mexico, after a sojourn on Staten Island, New York, left behind him a large lump of chicle gum. His landlord, Thomas Adams, came across it and thought it was some kind of rubber. He tried to vulcanise it – without success. He tried it as a base for false teeth, again a failure.

Then he remembered that the Mexican used always to be chewing it – and that he had lovely white teeth. So Adams sent some to a sweet shop and gained success at last. In 1871 he took out a patent for making chewing gum. Today in the United States 12,000,000 pounds of chicle gum is treated, with a retail value £23,000,000! In Great Britain one firm alone sells 1,000,000 packets a day during the summer.

In September 1867, the *New York Tribune* wrote under the title 'Santa Anna':

Since the Mexican war of independence, in 1821, there have been only two governments in the unhappy country on our south-west border against which Santa Anna has not headed an insurrection. Those two are Maximilian's and his own. He led the revolution which compassed the overthrow of Iturbide; rebelled against Pedraza in the interest of Guerrero; against Guerrero in the interest of Bustamente; against Bustamente as an ally of his old enemy Pedraza; and after holding the Presidency himself for several terms, went into exile in Cuba in 1845. He got back to Mexico by cheating the American government into the belief that he would favour the independence of Texas; but no sooner had he reached his capital than he raised his voice for war, and on the tide of national enthusiasm which the prospect of hostilities aroused, he was floated into the Presidency. The choice of another as his successor in this office while he was in the field against Scott and Taylor he over-ruled by the strong arm; and while his people entrusted him with the fortunes of their armies it is now known that he was secretly engaged in a fruitless negotiation with General Scott. Corrupt, wily, and unprincipled as he was, it is admitted that he was a soldier of no mean skill; but in the war with the United States he was signally beaten in all quarters, and before the conclusion of peace he resigned both his military and civil authority, and withdrew to Jamaica. Here he rested five years; but the old passion for intrigue and insurrection was strong upon him yet, and in the tumult of a revolution against President Arista he returned to power, plotted the destruction of his own constitution, and got up a new insurrection which declared him Most Serene Highness and President for life. Defeated by Alvarez after he had ruled with despotic power for two years, he was driven into banishment again in 1855, and went to the West Indies.

There are probably few Mexicans living who have done more mischief to their country, and are more cordially hated by the majority of their countrymen, than this scheming commander. Yet with all his unpopularity, and in spite of the unfortunate issue of all his political enterprises, he has never lost the hope of regaining the supreme control. In Cuba, in Venezuela, in St Thomas, on Staten Island, wherever he has lived during the twelve years of his exile, he has been constantly busy with new plots. His party, it is true, was small; but he had abundance of money, so he might hope to increase it.

Twice he has attempted to return, and each time he has been turned back by a foreign power. When the empire of Maximilian was established, he landed at Vera Cruz, and, licking the feet of the invaders, counselled the Mexicans, in a high-sounding proclamation, to yield a ready obedience to the European rulers. But Marshal Bazaine was too shrewd to accept the alliance of a man who had been all his life an unscrupulous plotter for power, and Santa Anna was instantly shipped to Havana. He came no more to Vera Cruz until the other day. How he was then a second time driven away from his native country by foreigners our readers know already; and much as we may regret the illegal conduct of the American naval commander on that occasion, there can be little question that Mexico has reaped profit from his mistake. Santa Anna has always been one of her worst enemies.

Of the ultimate fate of the unhappy old man who now at the age of nearly seventy has fallen a victim to his restless ambition we fear there can be little doubt. His seizure at Sisal by the liberals is almost equivalent to a sentence of death, for in the inflammation of passion which has followed their victory over the imperialists, and the hatred which they are known to cherish towards their prisoner, it is not likely that either law or justice will be very carefully considered. There may be no proof that the ex-dictator meditated interference with Mexican politics, or that he returned to his native land in any other capacity than that of a private citizen; but the prospect is that proof will not be waited for. Our last advices represented that a court-martial was about to assemble for his trial: our next despatches will probably announce his execution.

In May 1876, the *Cincinnati Enquirer* reported:

'General Santa Anna in his old age' – He lives in the City of Mexico, in a third-rate house of two stories, with courts of not more than twenty feet square, the pavements out of repair, the whole telling the story of poverty. He was seated upon a much-worn sofa, attended by a smart-appearing Mexican of middle age, and rose, with some difficulty, in receiving us. He complained considerably of his wooden leg, and also of blindness.

He is an old man of eighty years, very decrepit, yet in full command of his faculties; has a good head and face, not unlike the pictures of Humboldt in old age, with broad temples, and an abrupt square nose, and at one time good eyes. He had little to say, but appeared pleased at our visit; and, as we told him of the four or five general officers of the Mexican war still living, he listened with interest, but showed no special recognition until the name of Pillow was mentioned, whom he remembered perfectly.

127

Over the sofa where Santa Anna sat was the picture of a beautiful woman, in her fullness of youth and loveliness. This was his wife when both led the fortunes of Mexico. As we passed out the court our attention was called to the figure of a woman of fifty in the window opposite, in plain dress and devoid of any interesting attribute. This was she whose picture had so interested us, Mrs General Santa Anna.

Santa Anna married María Inés de la Paz García y Martínez de Uzcanga, the daughter of rich Spanish parents, in her home town of Alvarado in Vera Cruz, on 25 September 1825, when she was aged 13. She died on 23 August 1844; and on 8 October 1844, Santa Anna married María de los Dolores Diega Ignacia Tosta Gómez, when he was aged 50 and she was 17.

Antonio Lopez de Santa Anna died at his home in Mexico City, on 21 June 1876, aged 82, and was buried in a glass coffin with military honours at the Panteón Del Tepeyac Cemetery in Mexico City.

***

The centenary of the foundation of Texas in 1936 prompted a number of commemorative events. In June 1936 British newspapers reported: 'New Stamps for Texas – A special commemorative postage stamp has been issued by the United States Post Office to commemorate the centenary of the foundation in 1836 of the Independent Republic of Texas, now one of the United States. The stamps show the Alamo, the original State Building, and also portraits of Sam Houston and Stephen Austin. The stamps are inscribed United States postage Texas centennial and the dates 1836–1936. Special envelopes showing a map of Texas and two cowboys have also been issued to commemorate the centenary.'

On 28 July 1936, the remains of the defenders buried in the sanctuary of the Old San Fernando Church were exhumed and exposed to public view for a year. They were then entombed in a marble coffin on 11 May 1938, and on the same day a memorial plaque was erected in the church that records the events.

Eventually, the Alamo Cenotaph situated in front of the Alamo church facia on Alamo Plaza in San Antonio, known as 'the Spirit of Sacrifice' was begun at the time of the centenary and completed in 1939. It is made from grey Georgia marble and pink Texas granite. The San Antonio mayor at the time, Maury Maverick (1895–1954), held a dedication ceremony at the site on 11 November 1940. Inscribed on the stone are 187 names of those who were believed at that time to have fought at the Alamo.

The marker reads: 'Erected in memory of the Heroes who sacrificed their lives at the Alamo, March 6, 1836, in defense of Texas. They chose never to surrender nor retreat, these brave hearts with flag still proudly waving perished in the flames of immortality that the high sacrifice might lead to the founding of this Texas.'

On 18 December 1938, the Texas Centennial Commission erected a statue of James Butler Bonham on the courthouse square of the town of Bonham, which had been named in his honour.

Taylor County in Texas was named in honour of the three brothers who died at the Alamo, and in 1955 a bronze sculpture of them was unveiled at Abilene, having been sculptured by Lincoln Borglum, who was the son of the sculptor of Mount Rushmore.

As this publication goes to print, the construction of a world-class museum and visitor centre is under way to honour the shrine of Texas liberty.

***

Alamo-related themes have been remembered in books, pictures, films, songs and poems, with depictions of Davy Crockett on film and television outnumbering those of the actual battle. As time went by his name became overshadowed by the deeds of such Wild West legends as Buffalo Bill Cody, Wild Bill Hickok, Wyatt Earp, Jesse James, Billy the Kid, and many more. However, in 1873, the stage idol of the day, Frank Maguire Mayo (1839–96), brought Davy Crockett back to life in a boisterous Broadway melodrama based on incidents from Crockett's life in the backwoods, which became very popular. In 1909, a short silent film about Davy Crockett entitled *In Hearts United* was screened. It was written by Charles K. French (1860–1952), who also played the lead role.

The first film using the siege of the Alamo as the setting, *Martyrs of the Alamo*, also known as *The Birth of Texas*, appeared in 1915. It starred Sam DeGrasse (1875–1953), who played 'Deaf' Smith, known as 'Silent' Smith in the film. James Bowie was portrayed by the prolific London-born actor Alfred Paget (1879–1919). In the following year the popular silent film and theatre actor Dustin Farnum (1874–1929) depicted Davy Crockett in the first movie version of his life story, which was simply entitled *Davy Crockett*. In 1926 came *With Davy Crockett at the Fall of the Alamo*, with Crockett played by the well-known silent movie actor Cullen Landis (1896–1975).

Released on 16 September 1917, the silent film *The Conqueror* starred Bostonian William Farnum (1876–1953) as Sam Houston. *The Conqueror* is an R.A. Walsh production, and is screened with all the care and attention to detail that is so characteristic of Walsh pictures.

Houston's rapid rise to power from a rough frontiersman to governor of a state is one of the most vivid picture stories ever told, particularly the scenes concerning the battle of San Jacinto. Farnum received a star on the Hollywood Walk of Fame in 1960.

It is interesting to note that as Enrique Esparza lived until 1917 and Alijo Pérez Junior until 1918, they would probably have been aware of some of these productions.

The first song about the Alamo was recorded in late 1938 by Bob Wills and his Texas Playboys, which was entitled 'New San Antonio Rose'. This was followed on 24 September 1937 by the film *Heroes of the Alamo*, described as the 'Epic drama of the birth of great new state'. It starred little-known Texas-born actor Bruce Warren (1904–49) playing Almaron Dickinson, with Ruth Finlay (1896–1949) depicting his wife, Susanna. It includes a controversial scene of David Crockett trying to escape, and the defenders singing 'The Yellow Rose of Texas', although the song is not believed to have been written at the time of the battle.

As war clouds loomed over Europe, *Man of Conquest*, which was released on 15 May 1939, covered the life of Sam Houston and events before and after the Alamo, with Richard Dix (1893–1949) in the starring role. This was followed by Edwin Justus Mayer's 1941 play *Sunrise in My Pocket*.

Alamo-related themes had their most prolific time in the 1950s. In the first year of the decade the famous Hollywood actor George Montgomery (1916–2000) starred in the not very true to life film entitled *Davy Crockett: Indian Scout*. In 1952 came *The Iron Mistress*, based on the 1951 book of the same name by Paul I. Wellman. It is based on the life of James Bowie up to his marriage to Ursula de Veramendi. It starred Alan Ladd (1913–64) as Jim Bowie; and Virginia Mayo (1920–2005) as Judalon de Bornay – the Iron Mistress.

In 1954–55, as part of the Magical World of Disney, a five-part television series entitled *Davy Crockett* was aired, which starred 'Disney Legend' Fess Parker (1924–2010), a Texan who later played the role of Daniel Boone; and Buddy Ebsen (1908–2003), who later found fame as the much-loved Jed Clampett in *The Beverly Hillbillies*. They also starred in the Disney films that followed: *Davy Crockett: King of the Wild Frontier*, which was released on 25 May 1955, and *Davy Crockett and the River Pirates*, released on 18 July 1956. From this came 'The Ballad of Davy Crockett', which was performed by Fess Parker himself, included the immortal lines 'Davy, Davy Crockett, King of the Wild Frontier'. Parker is reported to have 'toppled Marlon Brando as the guest most in demand at Hollywood parties', and the racoon population is said to have decreased. Still believed to have been a real person who died at the Alamo, the fictional character of Thimblerig is a riverboat gambler played by Hans Conried in the 1955 film.

Film critic Alfred Wood wrote in the *World's News* for 26 November 1955, under the heading 'Davy Crockett Lives Again':

His coonskin cap and Ol' Betsy has swept him to the top as Number 1 pin-up boy for young America.

A rangy young backwoodsman, Indian fighter and fringed buckskin-dressed pioneer, has come back from the dusty pages of Wild West history to become the No. 1 pin-up character of millions of American boys and girls.

And, if early indications are any guide, he is likely to jump to the top in the eyes and minds of Australian children as well, in the near future.

The character is Davy Crockett, dead for the past 120 years, but suddenly resurrected on a US nationwide television program about 12 months ago.

Almost in a flash – it seems – he has swept Hopalong Cassidy and the various spaceman heroes from their pedestals faster than ducks in a shooting gallery.

Today, almost every boy and girl has discarded 10-gallon hats, six guns, ray projectors, and space helmets for the coonskin cap and muzzle loader Ol' Betsy that are the trademarks of their new found homespun hero, Davy Crockett.

The brain behind the reincarnation of Crockett is Walt Disney. But even Walt had no idea of what he was launching when he picked a 28-year-old Texan, Fess Parker, to play the part of Davy in one of a routine series of TV shorts glamorising some of the old-time pioneers of the West.

Fess, hitherto an unknown actor, playing in TV soap opera, woke up the morning after his first Davy Crockett show to find he had become overnight, young America's No.1 pin-up boy. Within a few weeks America became Crockett crazy.

The Ballad of Davy Crockett originally written by a Disney studio musician, as mere background music for the TV show, crashed the top of the nation's hit parades and has stayed there.

Leading vocalists have cashed in on the recording field. So far 16 different versions are on sale. Burl Ives, king of the folklore ballad mongers, topped the first million recordings sold, and still sells the most popular recording.

Only just in its first year, the Crockett craze has already netted more than 100 million dollars for those who jumped the Davy band wagon and cashed in on Crockett merchandise.

Youthful pioneers can be fitted out from underpants to fringed frontier jacket and kept happy for hours with gadgets and games all bearing the magic name of Davy Crockett.

The toy Tommy gun and ray disintegrator are now playthings of yesterday, giving place to the long-barrelled muzzle-loader, with the carved stock and complete with percussion cap mechanism, based on Davy's own famous weapon, Ol' Betsy, which has sold in hundreds of thousands.

Grandmothers, mothers and elderly aunts have been importuned into turning out wardrobes and attics in search of raccoon skin coats, moth-eaten maybe, but a treasure now. Once popular about the 20s, and long since despised, these furs have now jumped to mink and sable prices.

The shortage of skins for making the distinctive Davy Crockett cap has sent trappers out into the woods for the first time in years, and the raccoon, a tiny animal, not unlike the common Australian possum, is in danger of being wiped out forever.

Small boys and girls, too, in coonskin caps, lisping, 'Hi, pardner, my name's Davy', have become such a common sight throughout the length and breadth of the country that it is easy to understand a Michigan woman's consternation when she rang the police at 1 am to report that a young Davy was perched in a tree in front of her house and refused to come down. A policeman from a squad car hailed the young tree climber, but was ignored. The cop sent for the fire brigade with their searchlight, ladder and jumping net. When the firemen arrived, the intruder was found to be a real racoon – scared out of his wits by the glare and shouting – and probably alarmed at the rising demand for his skin and those of his fellows.

All this ballyhoo merely goes to show how the enthusiasm of 30 million TV viewers can turn a half-legendary, almost-forgotten character into a bigger nation-wide impact than the atom bomb – or Dr. Kinsey's first report.

However, when the television series and films reached Britain in 1956 it influenced the sale of imitation coon hats and bows and arrows, which had its negative points, as several newspapers reported in April 1956, under the title: 'Davy Crockett Menace': 'Indians on the warpath are worrying British parents. In the London area, bows and arrows have claimed at least 50 victims recently – small boys treated at hospitals or by doctors for injuries after Cowboy and Indian battles. Davy Crockett hero worship is blamed for it. The 'Daily Mail' reported today [17 April 1956] that six 'Crocketts lie injured in one London hospital.'

The Last Command, a film told through the perspective of James Bowie, was released on 3 August 1955, and starred the Second World War hero Sterling Hayden (1916–86) as Bowie, with the Oscar-nominated J. Carrol Naish (1896–1973) as Santa Anna.

The First Texan, released on 19 June 1956, was the second film that highlighted the exploits of Sam Houston, with Joel McCrea

(1905–90) in the starring role. *The Adventures of Jim Bowie* was an American television series that first aired on 7 September 1956, and ran for two years. It starred the English actor Conrad Scott-Forbes (1920–97), known as Scott Forbesm, who was an Oxford graduate.

The first epic and fully appreciated depiction of the battle – *The Alamo* – was released on 24 October 1960, and starred the Oscar-winning American movie legend John Wayne (1907–79), as Davy Crockett, who also directed the film; Oscar-nominated Richard Widmark (1914–2008) as Jim Bowie; and the Lithuanian-born noted English actor Laurence Harvey (1928–73) as William Barret Travis. The soundtrack to the movie included 'The Ballad of the Alamo', which was recorded by singer-songwriter Marty Robbins (1925–82) and became the most popular song about the battle.

The comedy farce *Viva Max* was released on 18 December 1969 and based on a novel of the same name, which itself was loosely based on the battle of the Alamo. It starred the London-born, Oscar-winning character actor Sir Peter Ustinov (1921–2004) as the Mexican leader General Maximilian Rodriguez de Santos – indeed, none of the characters bear the names of the real people who were involved in the conflict.

Released on 26 January 1987, *The Alamo: Thirteen Days to Glory* was a film that focused mainly on Colonel William Barret Travis. It was shot at the same location as the 1960 film, and starred Alec Baldwin (born in 1958) as Travis; with James Arness (1923–2011) as James Bowie. Arness later starred as Marshal Matt Dillon in the television western series *Gunsmoke*.

The Alamo was released on 9 April 2004 and starred Patrick Wilson (born in 1973) as William Barret Travis; Billy Bob Thornton (born in 1955) as Davy Crockett; and Jason Patric (born in 1966) as Jim Bowie. Although the screenplay tried to be as true to fact as possible, the film lost Touchstone Pictures millions of dollars. Nevertheless, it often appears among the various top fifty lists of great historical movies.

***

In November 1998, newspapers in Los Angeles, and around the world published the following under the title 'Diary challenges Alamo claims of heroic defeat':

> Two unidentified Texans paid $US350,000 for a diary that challenges one of the most popular legends in their state's history: that Davy Crockett proudly fought Mexican troops to the end of the thirteen-day siege at the Alamo.

The 200-page manuscript, purchased yesterday at an auction in Hollywood, is supposedly a Mexican army officer's eyewitness account of Crockett's death on 6 March 1836.

The controversial diary says the King of the Wild Frontier was captured and executed with other volunteers in the force of 200 who were defending the former Spanish mission in their fight to create the state of Texas out of Mexican territory.

Many experts doubt the account, said to have been dictated in Spanish in the 1840s by Lieutenant Colonel Jose Enrique de la Pena. It defies the traditional story of the Alamo's capture in which the volunteer force died on the walls or in hand-to-hand combat with General Antonio Lopez de Santa Anna's troops.

The traditional story holds that Crockett, the former congressman from Tennessee, fought to the end, wielding his long-rifle, 'Betsy' like a club before he fell near the front doors of the Alamo's chapel.

Little was known about the buyers other than that they purchased the diary through a New York dealer with the intent of keeping it in Texas, said Gregory Shaw, vice-president of Butterfield and Butterfield auction house.

Among critics of the diary is Joseph Musso, a Los Angeles-based historic illustrator, who is researching a biography on Alamo commander James Bowie. Musso questioned the validity of the documents because they seemed to surface out of nowhere in 1955 in the hands of a Mexican coin dealer. 'It doesn't have 110 years of human records behind it,' Musso said, asserting that not enough forensic tests have been conducted. Critics have dismissed de la Pena's memoir as a fake ever since an English translation by San Antonio archivist Carmen Perry was published in 1975.

Bill Groneman, a New York arson investigator, called the journal a forgery in his book, 'Defence of a Legend: Crockett and the de la Pena Diary.' He has acknowledged, however, that he cannot prove it.

But James Crisp, a history professor at North Carolina State University, has studied the documents and is convinced they are genuine. 'They have passed every test,' Crisp said yesterday. Shaw said the memoir was written on paper of high rag content, typical of the early nineteenth century.

The diary had been at the John Peace Library at the University of Texas at San Antonio for nearly 25 years, but was sold by John Peace, son of the man for whom the library was named.

Texans associate the Alamo with a great sense of patriotic pride, so many would be offended at the thought of Crockett surrendering.

The diaries, consisting of 200 loose pages, are now kept at the Centre for American History at the University of Texas in Austin.

***

Several British people have been associated with the Alamo over the years.

The Anglo-American prolific novelist Amelia E. Barr, who had lived in Texas for a few years, wrote a story in 1888 entitled 'Remember the Alamo'. She later turned it into a series, the chapters of which were published in several newspapers under the title 'For Faith and Freedom', which was about the Texas Revolution, and Chapter XIV was entitled 'The Fall of the Alamo'. It tells of the family of Jose Antonio Navarro, and although it is a dramatised and mainly fictitious account of the events, it is evident the author did some historical research and it captures the mood of the day.

London rock singer David Jones (1947–2016) was fascinated by American culture and Hollywood movies from a young age. In 1965 he decided to change his name to avoid clashing with Davy Jones, the Manchester-born frontman of the American popular music group The Monkees. He adopted the name David Bowie, in homage to Jim Bowie, the on-screen rebel played by Richard Widmark in the 1960 Alamo film. He became one of the most influential musicians of his era.

On 19 February 1982, Ozzy Osbourne, the Birmingham-born frontman of the British rock band Black Sabbath, while intoxicated and wearing a dress belonging to Sharon Arden, his future wife, because she had hidden his clothes, urinated on the Alamo cenotaph. A police officer arrested him and he was subsequently banned from performing in San Antonio for a decade. He was allowed back in 1992 after an apology and a donation of $10,000 to the Daughters of the Republic of Texas.

In February 1986, the year of the 150th anniversary, the Prince of Wales (now King Charles III) visited Texas, which one American newspaper reporter referred to disparagingly as 'a has-been republic – a nation that lasted only nine years and fizzled more than a century ago'. Charles visited the San Jacinto battlefield, and although he called in at San Antonio there is no report that he visited the Alamo.

However, during a visit to Texas in 1991, HM Queen Elizabeth II and Prince Philip went to the Alamo on 21 May and signed the visitors' book. In a newspaper article about the event it was said that the sovereign was very moved when she learned of those born in England who fought in the battle of the Alamo.

On 9 April 2010, Jim Mather, the then Scottish minister for Energy, Enterprise and Tourism, visited San Antonio, where he laid a commemorative handcrafted stone of Caithness marble at the Alamo shrine; the only time the Daughters of the Republic of Texas have allowed such an item to remain there permanently. The inscription reads: 'From the people of Scotland, in memory of the four native Scots, and the many other defenders of Scots ancestry, who gave their lives at the Alamo on March 6, 1836.'

The British rock musician Phil Collins has had a passion for the subject from a young age, and has a large collection of Alamo and Texiana artefacts. At a press conference held at the Alamo on 26 June 2014 he announced that he was to present his collection to the Alamo via the Texas General Land Office, who are guardians of the Alamo on behalf of the people of Texas. In appreciation of his donation, on 11 March 2015 he was named an honorary Texan by the State Legislature, and in 2023 the collection went on display in the Alamo Collections Centre in San Antonio.

11

'DON'T REMEMBER THE ALAMO!'

On 29 April 1994, under the heading: 'Don't Remember the Alamo', the *Voice of America* reporter Jamie Dettmer, stated:

> There is an old saying down in San Antonio, Texas – 'If there had been a back door at the Alamo there wouldn't have been any heroes.' Maybe it should be updated along the lines of, 'If Davy Crockett had heard of political correctness, he wouldn't have bothered to die for Texas independence.'
>
> More than a century after Crockett, Jim Bowie, Bill Travis and 184 other Americans sacrificed their lives to defend the mansion of San Antonio de Valero against 5000 Mexican troops, a new battle over the Alamo has erupted. The 'Deguclio', the Mexican bugle call for 'Death to the Defenders,' has been sounded again and prisoners are most certainly not being taken.
>
> The dispute over the Alamo this time is a three-cornered fight, pitching the formidable Daughters of the Texas Republic, who since 1905 have run the Alamo site, American-Mexican activists led by a mayoral wannabe, and the Inter-Tribal Council of American Indians. On paper, the modern defenders, the 6000 Daughters of the Texas Republic, are facing odds as great as any of those confronted by Bowie and his men. Hispanic Americans make up 56 per cent of the San Antonio electorate, and they seem ready to support a fresh look at the battle for the Alamo and the myths that Anglo-Texans hold dear and guard with fierce pride.
>
> As with the original battle, there has been much pre-conflict manoeuvring. Back in 1836, the Mexican forces led by President Antonio Lopez de Santa Anna laid siege on the mission for 10 days before hoisting a red flag signalling that no quarter should be given and sending in his columns. Bill Thornton, the San Antonio Davy Crockett, in coon-skin cap, in a detail from a painting at the Witt Memorial Museum, San

137

Antonio, Texas, city councilman leading the American-Mexicans, has not yet raised a red emblem but is poised at the bottom of the flag-staff ready to do so. Thornton has the backing of a new generation of mainly Hispanic historians, who recently have been questioning the valour of the men of the Alamo and the tales about them, tales which have played a crucial part in the memory of the foundation of Texas and its splitting away from Mexico.

Davy Crockett is now said never to have worn a coonskin cap. He wanted to surrender to the superior Mexican forces, it is argued. According to the new history, Bill Travis was mad from drinking mercury in an effort to cure a venereal disease. The men of the Alamo were not inspired by the idea of liberty but were just land-grabbing mercenaries.

This revised look at Texas history in some ways reflects a general political correctness trend sweeping across the states as a whole, one that has prompted a series of reassessments about the American past. But in Texas the current argument is not purely an academic one. If the new history wins out it could have practical results. The Alamo site could be wrested out of the control of the Daughters of the Texas Republic. For the Daughters, the Alamo is a national shrine celebrating the bravery of the men who followed Crockett and Bowie into the pages of established history (and into Hollywood movies). What is left of the site – the Alamo itself, the chapel of the old mission – is sacred and should not be tampered with, argue the ladies, who to join the Daughters are required to prove they are descendants of the original founders of the Texas Republic. For American-Mexicans, the Alamo is merely part of 'Anglo' mythology, and a chauvinist one at that, and the area around the old chapel should be renovated. Most Mexican-Americans see it more as a shrine to racism than as shrine to liberty, according to Avelardo Valdez, a University of Texas sociologist.

Thornton, who plans to run for mayor, is leading a campaign to restore the Alamo and the adjacent area and to point up the history of the mission in the years before the Alamo and the fight for Texas independence. Tourist information at the site should emphasise the Spanish-Mexican history of the mission before the 1836 battle. 'The doors have been opened,' he says. 'Places have been made at the table for people whose voices have not been heard before.' But political correctness can be a tricky thing, and three-cornered fights sometimes lead to odd and shifting alliances, as the Serbs can tell you.

Both the Daughters and the Hispanics have found a confusing ally – not the Seventh Cavalry, but the American Indian. After a few pow-wows, the Inter Tribal Council of American Indians criticised the Anglos' history of the Alamo but also expressed doubts about the renovation of the area adjacent to the old chapel. The Indians maintain there are graves of Indian converts to Christianity buried around the Alamo. The Inter-Tribal Council's intervention came in a dramatic way. The council's president arrived at the site brandishing an arrow and proclaiming: 'This is the arrow of truth, justice and historical fact.' He declared the site sacred ground. The city council felt moved to close the street outside the Alamo to stop tour buses running over possible graves. A committee has now been formed to determine what to do next. History used to be a lot easier. Can anyone see a back door?

As the title suggests, in their 2021 book *Forget the Alamo: the Rise and Fall of an American Myth,* three Texans devalue almost everything about the Alamo; with views that are almost exactly the opposite to those expressed in the introduction to this work. Its concentration on the politics of Texas and possible ulterior motives of the defenders has influenced the writers to disregard '... what those poor souls went through', and the enormous sacrifice they made. The book has been received by some as a new insight into the siege of the Alamo, and by others as an unforgivable slur on the history of Texas.

EXPLOITS AND ADVENTURES IN TEXAS

Exploits and Adventures in Texas was regarded for many years as a factual account of events at the Alamo, which was believed to have shed some light on Davy Crockett's Tennessee Mounted Volunteers. It was cited in scholarly work and was used as a source by film-makers. The series about the adventures of Davy Crockett, which was created by Disney in the 1950s, even reintroduced a character from the book named Thimblerig. However, it was a hoax!

While Davy Crockett's 1834 autobiography *A Narrative of the Life of David Crockett* had sold well in Britain, a second work published in 1835 and attributed to him entitled *An Account of Colonel Crockett's Tour to the North and Down East*, had fared not nearly as well. Therefore, with the frontiersman's unexpected death at the Alamo, his Philadelphia publishers, Carey and Abraham, sought to capitalise on the event and try to recoup their losses with the late summer 1836 release of Colonel Crockett's *Exploits and Adventures in Texas. Wherein is Contained a full Account of his Journey from Tennessee to the Red River and Natchitoches; and Thence Across Texas to San Antonio; Including his many hair breadth escapes; Together with a Topographical, Historical and Political View of Texas.*

However, although the book was said to have disingenuously been 'Written by Himself', the publishers had actually engaged a Philadelphia writer named Richard Penn Smith (1799–1854), who pieced together several of Crockett's congressional 1835 letters, along with observations from Mary Austin Holley's (1784–1846) Texas travel memoir, and passages from other Texas narratives with purely invented anecdotes, including excerpts from a 'journal' Crockett supposedly kept right up to the day before Mexican troops stormed the Alamo walls. The identity of the true writer was revealed in 1884.

In place of the real men who had fought and died with Crockett at the Alamo, *Exploits and Adventures* had the colonel travelling with four companions: Ned, a young bee hunter (a character borrowed from the work of James Fennimore Cooper (1789–1851) entitled *The Prairie*, one of his *Leather-stocking Tales*, which also included *The Last of the Mohicans*, an 1827 novel also published by Edward Carey; Thimblerig, a low gambler from Natchez who plied games of sleight; an Indian hunter; and an aging pirate.

Publishers have since reprinted *Exploits and Adventures* in conjunction with the legitimate narrative, and therefore spin-off accounts of Crockett's final exploits have often inserted this picaresque quartet in place of the men who actually accompanied him. This is unfortunate, as it diminishes the real men of the Tennessee Mounted Volunteers and obscures the motives behind those who launched the Texas Revolution; and it has without doubt been the source of some of the myths that have surrounded Crockett's life.

Under the title: 'The Thimble Conjuror of the Mississippi', several newspapers around the British Empire published the following 'droll incident' taken from Colonel Crockett's *Exploits and Adventures in Texas:*

There was a considerable number of passengers on board the Mississippi steamer, and our assortment was like the Yankee merchant's cargo of notions pretty particularly miscellaneous, I tell you. I moved through the crowd from stem to stern, to see if I could discover any face that was not altogether strange to me; but after a general survey, I concluded that I had never seen one of them before. There were merchants, and emigrants, and gamblers, but none who seemed to have embarked in the particular business that for the time being occupied my mind. I could find none who were going to Texas. All seemed to have their hands full enough of their own affairs, without meddling with the cause of freedom. The greater share of glory will be mine, thought I; so go ahead, Crockett.

I saw a small cluster of passengers at one end of the boat, and hearing an occasional burst of laughter, thinks I, there's some sport started in that quarter; and having nothing better to do, I'll go in for my share of it. Accordingly, I drew nigh to the cluster, and seated on a chest was a tall lank sea-serpent looking black-leg, who had crawled over from Natchez, and was amusing the passengers with his skill at thimblerig. At the same time he was picking up their shillings just about as expeditiously as a hungry gobbler would a pint of corn. He was doing what might be called an average business in a small way, and lost no time in gathering up the fragments. I watched the whole process for some time, and found that he had adopted the example set by the old Tempter himself, to get the weather-gage of us poor weak mortals. He made it a point to let his victims win always the first stake, that they might be tempted to go ahead; and then when they least suspected it, he would come down them like a hurricane in a corn-field, sweeping all before it.

I stood looking on, seeing him pick up the food from the greenhorns, and thought the men were fools to be cheated out of their hard earnings by a fellow who had just brains enough to pass a pea from one thimble to another, with such sleight of hand that you could not tell under which he had deposited it. The thimble conjuror saw me looking on, and eyeing me as if he thought I would be a good subject, said carelessly: 'Come, stranger, won't you take a chance?' the whole time passing the pea from one thimble to the other, by way of throwing out a bait for the gudgeons to bite at.

'I never gamble, stranger,' says I; 'principled against it; think it a slippery way of getting through the world at best.'

'Them are my sentiments to a notch,' says he; 'but this is not gambling, by no means a little innocent pastime, nothing more. Better take a buck by way of trying your luck at guessing.'

All this time he continued working with his thimbles; first putting the pea under one, which was plain to be seen, and then uncovering it, would show that the pea was there; he would then put it under the second thimble, and do the same, and then under the third; all of which he did to show how easy it would be to guess where the pea was deposited, if one would only keep a sharp look-out.

'Come, stranger,' says he to me again, 'you had better take a chance. Stake a trifle, I don't care how small, just for the fun of the thing.'

'I am principled against betting money,' says I; 'but I don't mind, going in for drinks for the present company, for I'm as dry as one of little Isaac Hill's regular set-speeches.'

'I admire your principles,' says he; 'and to show that I play with these here thimbles just for the sake of pastime, I will take that bet, though I'm a whole hog temperance man. Just say when, stranger.'

He continued all the time slipping the pea from one thimble to another; my eye was as keen as a lizard's, and when he stopped, I cried out: 'Now the pea is under the middle thimble.'

He was going to raise it, to show that it wasn't there, when I interfered, and said: 'Stop, if you please,' and raised it myself, and sure enough the pea was there; but it might have been otherwise if he had had the uncovering of it.

'Sure enough you've won the bet,' says he. 'You've a sharp eye, but I don't care if I give you another chance. Let us go fifty cents this bout; I'm sure you'll win.'

'Then you're a fool to bet, stranger,' says I, 'and since that is the case, it would be little better than picking your pocket to bet with you; so I'll let it alone.'

'I don't mind-running the risk,' said he.

'But I do,' says I, 'and since I always let well enough alone, and I have had just about glory enough for one day, let us all go to the bar and liquor.'

This called forth a loud laugh at the thimble conjuror's expense; and he tried hard to induce me to take just one chance more, but he might just as well have sang psalms to a dead horse, for my mind was made up; and I told him that I looked upon gambling as about the dirtiest way a man could adopt to get through this dirty world; and that I would never bet anything beyond a quart of whiskey upon a rifle tot, which I considered a legal bet, and gentlemanly and rational amusement.

'But all this cracking,' says I, 'makes me very thirsty; so let us adjourn to the bar and liquor.'

He gathered up his thimbles, and the whole company followed us to the bar, laughing heartily at the conjuror; for, as he had won some of their money, they were sort of delighted to see him beaten with his own cudgel.

He tried to laugh, too, but his laugh wasn't at all pleasant, and rather forced. The bar-keeper placed a big-bellied bottle before us; and after mixing our liquor, I was called on for a toast by one of the company, a chap just about as rough hewn as if he had been cut out of a gum log by a broad axe, and sent into the market without even being smoothed off with a jack plane – one of them chaps who, in their journey through life, are always ready for a fight or a frolic, and don't care the toss of a copper which.

'Well, gentlemen,' says I, 'being called on for a toast, and being in a slave-holding state, in order to avoid giving offence, and running the risk of being lynched, it may be necessary to premise that I am neither an abolitionist nor anti-abolitionist, but simply Colonel Crockett of Tennessee, now bound for Texas.'

When they heard my name, they gave three cheers for Colonel Crockett; and silence being restored, I continued: 'Now, gentlemen, I will offer you a toast, hoping, after what I have stated, that it will give offence to no one present; but should I be mistaken, I must imitate the old Roman, and take the responsibility. I offer, gentlemen, "the abolition of slavery:" Let the work begin in the two houses of Congress.'

They drank the toast in a style that satisfied me, that the little magician might as well go to a pigsty for wool, as to beat round in that part for voters; they were all either for Judge White or Old Tippecanoe. The thimble conjuror having asked the bar-keeper how much was to pay, was told there were sixteen smallers; which amounted to one dollar, and he immediately laid down the blunt in one of Biddle's notes.

After setting my face against gambling, Thimblerig was obliged to break off conjuring for want of customers, and call it half a day. He came and entered into conversation with me, and I found him a good-natured intelligent fellow, with a keen eye for the main chance. He belonged to that numerous class that it is perfectly safe to trust as far as a tailor can sling a bull by the tail – but no further. He told me that he had been brought up a gentleman; that is to say, that he was not instructed in any useful pursuit by which he could obtain a livelihood, so that when he found he had to depend upon himself for the necessaries of life, he began to suspect that Dame Nature would have conferred a particular favour, if she had consigned him to the care of anyone else.

Idleness being the mother of all mischief, he had soon taken to very indifferent courses for livelihood: in short, he commenced the profession of swindler at Natchez. Here he remained till Judge Lynch began his practice in that quarter. This drove him to his shifts in the steam-boats on the river. I asked him to give me an account of Natchez, and his adventures there, and I would put it in the book I intended to write, when he gave me the following, which betrays that his feelings were still somewhat irritated at being obliged to give them leg-bail when Judge Lynch made his appearance. I give it in his own words:

'Natchez is a land of fevers, alligators, n-----s, and cotton bales: where the sun shines with force sufficient to melt the diamond, and the word ice is expunged from the dictionary, for its definition cannot be comprehended by the natives; where to refuse grog before breakfast would degrade you below the brute creation; where the evergreen and majestic magnolia-tree, with its superb flower, unknown to the northern climes, and its fragrance unsurpassed, calls forth the admiration of every beholder; and the dark moss hangs in festoons from the forest trees, like the drapery of a funeral pall; where bears, the size of young jackasses, are fondled in lieu of pet dogs; and knives, the length of a barber's pole, usurp the place of Tooth-picks; where the filth of the town is carried off by buzzards, and the inhabitants are carried off by fevers; and where nigger women are knocked down by the auctioneer. Such is Natchez.

'The town is divided into two parts, as distinct in character as they are in appearance, Natchez-on-the-Hill, situated upon a high bluff overlooking the Mississippi, is a pretty little town, with streets regularly laid out and ornamented with divers handsome public buildings. Natchez-under-the-Hill – where, o where, shall I find words suitable to describe the peculiarities of that unholy place?

'An odd affair occurred while I was last there,' continued Thimblerig. 'A steam-boat stopped at the landing, and one of the hands went ashore under the hill to purchase provisions, and the adroit citizens of that delectable retreat, contrived to rob him of all his money. The captain of the boat, a determined fellow, went ashore in the hope of persuading them to refund – but that wouldn't do. Without further ceremony, assisted by his crew and passengers, some three or four hundred in number, he fastened an immense cable to the frame tenement where the theft had been perpetrated, and allowed fifteen minutes for the money to be forthcoming; vowing, if it was not produced within that time, to put steam to his boat, and drag the house into the river. The money was instantly produced.

'I witnessed a sight during my stay there,' continued the thimble conjuror, 'that almost froze my heart with horror, and will serve as a specimen of the customs of the far south. A planter of the name of Forster, connected with the best families of the state, unprovoked, in cold blood murdered his young and beautiful wife, a few months after marriage. He beat her deliberately to death in a walk adjoining his dwelling, carried the body to the hut of one of his slaves, washed the dirt from her person, and, assisted by his negroes, buried her upon his plantation. Suspicion was awakened, the body disinterred, and the villain's guilt established. He fled, was overtaken, and secured in prison. His trial was, by some device of the law, detained until the third term of the court. At length it came on; and so clear and indisputable was the evidence, that not a doubt was entertained of the result; when, by an oversight on the part of the sheriff, who neglected swearing into office his deputy who summoned the jurors, the trial was abruptly discontinued, and all proceedings against Foster were suspended, or rather ended.

'There exists, throughout the extreme south, bodies of men who style themselves Lynchers. When an individual escapes punishment by some technicality of the law, or perpetrates an offence not recognised in courts of justice, they seize him, and inflict such chastisement as they conceive adequate to the offence. They usually act at night, and disguise their persons. This society at Natchez embraces all the lawyers, physicians, and principal merchants of the place. Foster, whom all good men loathed as a monster unfit to live, was called into court, and formally dismissed. But the Lynchers were at hand. The moment he stepped from the courthouse, he was knocked down, his arms bound behind him; his eyes bandaged, and in this condition was marched to the rear of the town, where a deep ravine afforded a fit place for his punishment. His clothes were torn from his back, his head partially scalped: they next bound him to a tree; each Lyncher was supplied with a cow-skin whip, and they took turns at the flogging, until the flesh hung in ribbons from his body. A quantity of heated tar was then poured over his head, and made to cover every part of his body: they finally showered a sack of feathers on him; and in this horrid guise, with no other apparel than a miserable pair of trousers, with a drummer at his heels, he was paraded through the principal streets at mid-day. No disguise was assumed by the Lynchers; the very lawyers employed upon his trial took part in his punishment.

'Owing to long confinement his gait had become cramped, and his movements were very filtering. By the time the procession reached the most public part of the town, Foster fell down from exhaustion, and was allowed to lie there for a time, without exciting the sympathies of any on an object of universal detestation. The blood oozing from his stripes had become mixed with the feathers and tar, and rendered his aspect still more horrible and loathsome. Finding him unable to proceed further, a common dray was brought, and with his back to the horse's tail, the drummer standing over him, playing the 'Rogue's March', he was reconducted to prison, the only place at which he would be received. A guard was placed outside of the jail, to give notice to this body of Lynchers when Foster might attempt to escape, for they had determined on branding him on the forehead, and cutting his ears off. At two o'clock in the morning of the second subsequent day, two horsemen with a lead-horse stopped at the prison, and Foster was with difficulty placed astride. The Lynchers wished to secure him; he put spurs to his beast, and passed them. As he rode by, they fired at him; a bullet struck his hat, which was knocked to the ground, and he escaped, but if ever found within the limits of the state, he will be shot down as if a price were set on his head.

'Sights of this kind,' continued Thimblerig, 'are by no means infrequent. I once saw a gambler, a sort of friend of mine, by the way, detected cheating at faro, at a time when the bets were running high. They flogged him almost to death, added the tar and feathers, and placed him aboard a dugout, a sort of canoe, at twelve at night; and with no other instruments of navigation than a bottle of whiskey and a paddle, set him adrift on the Mississippi. He has never been beard of since, and the presumption is that he either died of his wounds, or was run down in the night by a steamer. And this is what we call Lynching in Natchez.'

Thimblerig had also been at Vicksburg in his time and entertained as little liking for that place as he did for Natchez. He had luckily made his escape a short time before the recent clearing out of the sleight-of-hand gentry; and he reckoned some time would elapse before he paid them another visit. He said they must become more civilised first. All the time he was seated on a chest, and playing mechanically with his peas and thimbles, as if he were afraid he would lose the sleight, unless he kept his hand in constant practice. Nothing of any consequence occurred on our passage down the river, and I arrived at Natchitoches in perfect health, and in good spirits.

For the record, although only four of its members were actually from Tennessee, Captain William B. Harrison formed a company known as the Tennessee Mounted Volunteers at Nacogdoches, on 14 January 1836, and they reached the Alamo on 9 February 1836. The following are the members of the unit who are known to have accompanied Davy Crockett into the Alamo:

From Ohio
Captain William B. Harrison – aged 25
James Madison Rose – aged 31 (He was a nephew of President James Maddison; and a brother-in-law to David P. Cummins, one of the 'Immortal 32')

From Tennessee
Lieutenant Robert Campbell – aged 26
David Crockett – aged 49 (He was a cousin of another defender named John Harris)
Joseph Bayliss – aged 28
Micajah Autry – aged 43

From Logan County, Kentucky
Peter James Bailey III – aged 24 (Bailey County in Texas was named after him)
Daniel W. Cloud – aged 21
William Keener Fauntleroy – aged 22
(Benjamin) Archer (Martin) Thomas – aged 18
Joseph G. Washington – aged 28 (may have gone by the name of James Morgan)

From Mifflin County, Pennsylvania
William McDowall – aged 43
(Doctor) John Purdy Reynolds – aged 29 (His medical books are on display at the Alamo)

From Virginia
Richard L. Stockton – aged 19

Others
Major Jacob Roth
I.L.K. Harrison (Colonel Neill signed an affidavit in 1838 swearing that Harrison was a member of the garrison, and to his knowledge Harrison was killed in the battle of the Alamo.)

Appendix II

TEXAS

Robert Montgomery Martin (1801–68) was an Anglo-Irish historical writer and statistician, whose work on colonial matters was highly respected. A founder member of the Colonial Society in 1837, he was the editor of the London-based *Colonial Magazine and Commercial Maritime Journal* from 1840 to 1842. On 13 January 1841, two months after the British government formerly acknowledged Texas independence, he published an article in his magazine simply entitled 'Texas'. It is somewhat Anglophile, and 'what's in it for us', but it is worth presenting here because it gives his interpretation of the British view of the new republic's progress in its first five years of existence, how he believed Britain had influenced it, and made note of Britain's continued anti-slavery stance:

> On the 16th of November last, England formerly acknowledged the independence of the Republic of Texas. In making that acknowledgement, Lord Palmerston acted wisely as well as boldly. The independence of a country, and its ability to maintain that independence, are simple questions of fact, which, when answered affirmatively, give, by general consent of mankind, to the new country the right of demanding the acknowledgement, and imposes upon old countries the duty of acknowledging those facts, without reference or enquiry into the domestic institutions of the country seeking to be inserted on the roll of nations. This we take to be the true doctrine and usage of the law of nations. That Texas is de facto independent of Mexico cannot be denied. Its independence has been acknowledged by the United States, by France, Holland and Belgium, and, whether acknowledged by England or not, the fact of independence still exists. But, independently of this view of the subject of the law, which is unanswerable, the prompt acknowledgment of the independence of Texas, and the establishment of commercial relations with her at this moment, evinces great political wisdom on the part of our government.

England can now, as we understand she has done, offer her friendly mediation to settle the difficulties between Mexico and Texas – which offer has been accepted by the latter. This is not only an act of humanity on the part of the British government, but it will promote and generally add to the security of British interests in Mexico. For let us suppose that Texas were to invade Mexico with an army of 20,000 men, and dictate to her peace under the walls of her capital (and Texas has the power, and does not lack the courage, to achieve this), in such a conflict, British interests must suffer in common with all other interests in that country. Or let us suppose, what is still more probable, (Texas having seven vessels of war and Mexico none), that the young republicans were to blockade every port of the mother-country on the Gulf of Mexico, what would become of British commerce and property there?

If it be answered that England, not having recognized the independence of Texas, would not be bound to regard the blockade, we reply that the fact that the independence of Texas, acknowledged by the rest of the world, whether England acknowledges it or not, and that existing, she has no right to treat Texas as though it did not exist, and, although the Navy of Texas might be powerless before the mistress of the seas, yet she would not want friends to aid her in a just cause, even against England, and thus we might bring upon ourselves a 'Western question' which balls and shells and British gallantry might not settle so rapidly or satisfactorily as they have settled the 'Eastern question'. Besides, we understand that Texas voluntarily, and to her honour, offered to take upon herself a portion of the foreign debt of Mexico, amounting to £1,000,000 upon the establishment of peace with Mexico within six months, through the mediation of Her Majesty's government – a proportion of the entire debt of Mexico, much larger than the extent of the territory of Texas, its population, or resources, would warrant the legal or moral imposition of. This offer has, we believe, been made by Texas from a high sense of justice, and not from the slightest apprehensions of the hostilities or the power of Mexico, but, be that as it may, Lord Palmerston has secured that sum for British subjects, in the event of success attending his Pacific interference. Nor is this a small matter, when we consider the bad faith with which Mexico has acted towards the British-Mexican bond holders.

Many interesting considerations present themselves upon the introduction of this new member into the family of nations – all pointing to the wisdom and policy of recognition by England, if, indeed, they do not prove that she ought to have been the first to recognise Texas is larger than France; its soil is said to be unsurpassed by any in the world, and its climate admirably adapted to the European constitution. It is capable of producing more cotton than all the United States, of a better quality, and at a cheaper rate. Sugar can also be cultivated to great advantage; and all the grains, and fruits, and vegetables of Europe can be raised in great abundance. It is the only country in America where cotton and sugar can be extensively cultivated by white labour. Hides, tallow, beef, furs, pelt, live oak and cedar timber can also be exported to any extent. The inhabitants are intelligent, bold, hardy, enterprising and industrious, of the Anglo-American race. They have formed a government modelled after that of the United States, except that it is a single sovereignty of familiar interests, instead of a federative system of different interests which gives it prospects of greater permanency, efficiency, and simplicity, and renders it more acceptable to European tastes and notions.

By the constitution they have declared the African slave-trade piracy; they have established religious tolerance, and made all equal before the law. They have adopted the common law of England, and the laws are promptly and impartially administered. Religious and literary institutions are springing up in all directions and are liberally endowed by the government. Emigration is pouring into the country with unprecedented rapidity. Society is improving; and the English language, literature, and civilization, and spreading with railroad rapidity over scenes which were five short years ago, a wilderness.

The people of Texas have wisely established a very cheap government; the debt of the republic amounts only to about £600,000; and she has an un-appropriated public domain of 150,000,000 acres; intrinsically as valuable as any land in the world. This source, with the most reduced scale of taxes, will support the government for a century. It will not, therefore, be necessary to raise a revenue by imposts from foreign manufacturers, and having no manufactures of her own to protect, as the United States have – and not likely to have many for years to come, if ever – Texas may be said to be in a more favourable condition for an experiment of a perfectly free trade than any other country in the world.

All she asks is to send her immense products of the raw material, which we most need, and to receive in payment, free of duty, an immense and continually increasing amount of all our manufactures. We say all, because it must be remembered, the people of that country are our descendants, who have been educated with the same tastes and wants as ourselves. This quantity too, will be greatly increased to supply the northern Mexican states, British commerce with Mexico being greatly impeded by a high scale of import duties. In fact, if proper friendly relations with this young republic are promoted and encouraged by our government and people, Texas will present to England most of the advantages of a most prosperous colony, without any of the disadvantages resulting from colonial dependence.

The prosperity and advancement of Texas have also a political bearing of the highest interest. We have before stated that there is in the republic more land adapted to the cultivation of cotton than in all the United States, owing to the difference of climate and soil; more

150

cotton to the acre, of a better quality, and at a cheaper rate, can be there raised, than in the most favoured parts of the Union; add to this the fact that Texas will receive from England all her supplies free of duty, and, consequently, a great deal cheaper than the same supplies cost the cotton producers of the United States, where they are burdened with a heavy tariff; and it becomes evident that in a competition for the supply of the cotton markets in Europe, Texas can undersell her neighbours. Now the inevitable consequence of this will be to bring about a modification of the United States tariff laws or dissolution of the Union. The latter, we do not think likely to occur, but a modification of the tariff must take place through the influence which Texas, if encouraged, will immediately exercise over the Union of the States. We need not enlarge upon the advantages to our commercial and manufacturing interests, which must result from this rivalry and competition between our trans-Atlantic brethren.

Texas is also by nature an agricultural country, that she never can become a maritime power of any consequence; all her carrying trade will therefore be done by others. For this employment of commercial marine, England stands on the footing of the most favoured nation. From these reasons, hastily thrown together, it is clear that our government have acted wisely in acknowledging the independence of Texas; and we think in the interests and policy of Great Britain to do everything in her power to advance the prosperity and importance of the young republic. The indomitable spirit and power of the Saxon race is there, and only want encouragement to accomplish great results in a short time. The past history of the Texans, brief though it is, is in earnest of what they will hereafter achieve.

Five years ago Texas was a wilderness, inhabited by only thirty or forty thousand people. Their rights and charters were violated, and a military despotism attempted to be forced upon them. They resisted; and their territory was invaded by 8,000 men, under Santa Anna, the president of Mexico. In every action – and they had many – the Texans were victorious, no matter how great the disparity of numbers. Perhaps one action only ought to be termed victorious on their part; 182 men in a fort were attacked by Santa Anna, at the head of 8,000 troops; they refused all terms and maintained the contest for ten days, killing 1,500 Mexicans; and when at last overwhelmed by numbers, a woman, whose life was spared, relates that no Texan asked for quarter. She saw the last of the gallant band fall while raising the butt-end of his musket against a host. The children of these heroes have been adopted, and are educated by the state. A few months, however, saw Santa Anna's whole army routed and himself a prisoner; and though he had amply forfeited his life by his atrocities, he was liberated, as were all the Mexican prisoners.

Since then there has not been a hostile Mexican in Texas, and, so far as human foresight can predict, there never will be again. The friendly

Mexicans remaining in Texas amount to 500. Since the war Texas has increased her population, by emigration, to between 300,000 and 500,000. She has put the machinery of a well-organised government into complete operation; farms are opening, towns building, and everything wears the aspect of prosperity, with a go-ahead stamped on it. These are the people to produce what we want, and to consume what we manufacture. No country at present seems to present greater inducements for the employment of capital, or for emigration. The only serious object raised against Texas is the existence of slavery. On this subject, although we are not advocates of slavery, we think it proper to make a few suggestions.

That the existence of slavery is an evil to any country in which it is tolerated is a truth which few American slaveholders themselves deny. How to eradicate this evil is a question deeply interesting to humanity. The very sympathy felt for the condition of the negro is apt to excite an unjust prejudice against the slave-holder, and this too frequently generates a disregard of the difficulties of the slave-holder's situation, and the sacrifices he must make to indulge that humanity which the abolishment glories in without difficulty or sacrifice. It is only with the consent and by the co-operation of the slave-holder that slavery in the United States can be abolished; denunciation and abuse but rivet the chains of their slaves, which was instanced in the memorable case of the State of Kentucky, there the violent inference of the abolitionists actually prevented the emancipation contemplated by the slave-owners themselves. In order to bring about any harmony of action for the benefit of the Negro, it is of great importance to remove, as far as possible, that prejudice which prevents the slave-holder and abolitionist from reasoning together, or adopting some plan in unison, for the accomplishment of an object which all consider desirable.

The present population of the United States is certainly not responsible for the introduction of slavery into that country. They are indebted to their Dutch and English ancestors for that curse and its consequences; for it is an historical fact that the North American colonies remonstrated, and petitioned the crown over and over again, against the introduction of slaves into the country – but they remonstrated and petitioned in vain.

The fact that Great Britain made compensation for the negroes she liberated, sanctions and confirms the general idea that slaves are property, and so they are regarded in the United States, and so recognised in their constitutions and laws. Now let us suppose that all preliminary difficulties were removed, and consent obtained for universal emancipation, the first important question that would arise on the proposal of emancipation would be its cost. There are now probably 400,000 slaves in the United States, each worth on average £100, making the aggregate value of £400,000,000! But that is not all. If it be not wished to make freedom a curse to the Negroes, they must be removed from the country. It is impossible under present feelings, that the two races can exist in peace together as equals; there can be no amalgamation – no political equality.

The good, if not the existence of Negroes requires then, that they, when emancipated, should be removed. This expense, supposing a country could be procured free of cost, would, we suppose, amount to £10 per head, or £40,000,000, making a total of £440,000,000, or about one half the national debt of England, and this to be assumed from motives of humanity, by a country which has no debt. But even this is not the extent of the sacrifice, for all those employments in the United States which require combination of labour, and which are now performed by slaves, would be at an end, until the necessary combination of white labour, with a security for its uninterrupted continuance, could be procured. In fact, the difficulties in the way of the abolition of slavery in the United States, by means of compensation, appear insuperable. And to those who taunt the Americans with the example of England, we suggest that the cases are not analogous. England indulged her humanity at a cost of £20,000,000 – the same indulgence would cost the United States £440,000,000 – while the ability of England to pay £440,000,000 is as great as that of America to pay £20,000,000.

The English parliament did not represent the West Indian planter, or it might never have passed the emancipation act. The law that liberates the slave in America must be passed by the slave-holder himself, and those representing slave-holders. Those who passed the emancipation act were surrounded by the best domestic servants in the world, and able to command any amount of the cheapest labour, for any purpose required; in fact, they suffered no inconvenience from the act, but the contribution, as citizens, of their proportion of the £20,000,000; while the Americans, by an act of emancipation, besides the enormous contributions in money, would deprive themselves of labourers and domestic servants until that want can be permanently supplied by white labour. Now, such a supply they can only rely on by devising some plan to keep up the stream of emigration. It has been ascertained by experience, that slave labour is more expensive than white labour; consequently, the Negro is not kept in slavery so much for the economy of his labour, as that, being a slave, you can command his services when required, in countries where labour is scarce and difficult to be procured. If, then, the requisite amount of white labour, which is cheaper, can be furnished, the value of the slave, as property, is diminished or destroyed and in proportion as this is effected, the sum which would have to be paid for the emancipation of the slave is also diminished. If a sufficient amount of surplus labour of Europe could be transferred to the United States , the emigrant would not only be greatly benefited in their condition, but America would be supplied with an abundance of cheaper and better labour than that of slaves, this without injury to the slave-holder, would render the slaves valueless as property. Slave-owners would then liberate their slaves, and the only expense necessary to rid the United States of the curse of slavery, would be that of transporting them to some country where they could enjoy their freedom.

The question then occurs, how is this free supply of labour for the United States to be obtained? American has a boundless domain of most fertile waste lands, from which she derives a large revenue, even at the low price at which they are sold; but these lands are of less value to any individual purchaser than they would be if he, and all others had been required to pay four times the sum they did pay for them, provided the government had expanded one-half of this enhanced price in introducing labourers into the country, and the government at the same time would receive double the amount of revenue. If then the United States would fix permanently the price of her public lands at not less than 20 shillings per acre, one-fourth of the sum received would bring her in the same revenue she now receives, and three-fourths of the sum received might be applied to purposes of immigration. This would soon supply an abundance of labour, the high price of land would render it necessary that the labourer should work for hire for some years before he could indulge a propensity, which seems to be natural to man of acquiring property in the soil on which he resides; and when he did indulge that propensity, he would furnish the means of introducing another labourer into the country in his place, and thus the supply would be kept up. If this system could be once adopted in the United States, general emancipation would gradually, but certainly, follow; and a part of the fund arising from the sales of the public lands might, as required, be appropriated to removing the negroes, and thus the great object of emancipation might be accomplished without diminishing the revenue of the government, and without violation of the rights of private property; while the welfare of Europe would be promoted at the same time.

Why may not America declare every child born after a given time, free? The longer the present evil continues, the more difficult will be its removal – but while we are alternately moved by hopes and doubts and apprehensions in contemplating this vast complicated subject, we feel somewhat encouraged by the belief that we may call the serious attention of our brethren of the United States to this subject, by being instrumental in having the experiment made of the plan we have suggested, in a country where fortunately the subject is yet unencumbered by the appalling difficulties which surround the United States; we mean in the young republic of Texas, where unfortunately slavery has likewise been enacted. But before touching this part of the subject, we feel bound to state the extenuating circumstances attending the admission of slavery into Texas, still re-asserting our sincere regret that our brethren of Texas should have done an act so injurious to themselves, and which, we think, requires all the extenuation which truth will warrant.

When the revolution commenced in Texas, there were not more than thirty or forty thousand people in the country; they were poor and industrious, and had no slaves, they were emigrants from the southern and western (slave-holding) states of the American Union. There they had left their early associates – their friends and relations. The first reply which Mexico made to the revolution was to invade the country with 8,000 men, led on by Santa Anna, the president of the republic, calling himself the 'Napoleon of the West.' Santa Anna actually dispersed the convention which formed the present constitution of Texas – and burnt the little town of Washington, in which the convention sat. By that constitution slave-trade was declared to be piracy. Not a single voice was raised against its constitutional denunciation of piracy, and the public sentiment of the country would strongly co-operate with the fundamental law of the land, in inflicting the extreme penalties of the law on any who should dare to violate the law. The question of admitting slaves from the United States was much discussed. It was contended, that being slaves in the United States, their admission as such did not increase the number of slaves in the world, while their removal to a better climate and a more abundant country must naturally improve their condition.

But more power than these arguments was the fact that a few daring men in Texas had, by resistance to oppression, defied the power of Mexico, and drawn down upon themselves an invading army of 8,000 men. In contest against such fearful odds they received sympathy alone from their slave-holding friends and relations in the United States; from them alone could they expect the assistance of stout hearts and strong arms in the impending conflict; but these men could not be expected to emigrate to Texas and participate in its perilous fortunes unless they were permitted to bring with them their domestic slaves, and to have that sort of property guaranteed to them by the constitution. Under these circumstances, that a convention, representing a people without slaves, should permit others to emigrate to the country with slaves, shows that they were influenced in doing so by a sort of moral necessity, which, while it cannot, in our opinion, justify, must be admitted to extenuate the fault of such admission, so far, at least, as to remove a portion of that prejudice which now prevents so many good men in this country from co-operating in some practical plan for the removal of an evil they so much deprecate.

It will soon be apparent that Lord Palmerston has secured to our government great moral influence with the young republic of Texas, by wisely abstaining from the assertion of any right to interfere in her domestic institutions – even in that of slavery; and as there are said to be only 5,000 slaves yet in Texas, and consequently that a large majority of the population can have no interest in favour of the continuance of that evil, we think the time and the circumstances peculiarly favourable for a friendly effort on our part, to induce the Texans to put a stop to this evil.

We write upon the presumption, which we believe to be true, that the people of Texas look upon slavery as an evil which it is desirable to rid them of, and which they want of sufficient white labour alone prevents them from abolishing. If this be true, and if it also be true, as we believe it is, that history affords no example of a civilised country in which land was cheap and slavery did not exist – or of a country where land was dear and slavery did exist – may we not hope to induce the congress of Texas to fix a permanent high minimum price upon all their public lands, and to expend a portion of that fund in procuring emigrants from Europe, and so get rid of slavery. This, we believe, can be accomplished; and when accomplished, it would be an example which might lead to the most glorious results in the United States, where a similar experiment almost needs the encouragement of assured success, to induce men to encounter the difficulties which oppose themselves to emancipation in the Union.

With these feelings, opinions, and anticipations, we say to our countrymen, abolitionists, and all – discard your prejudices – cultivate the most intimate and friendly relations with Texas – promote her prosperity – encourage emigration to her shores – be indulgent to what you think her faults, and point out to her, in a friendly spirit, what you think her interests and her honour require – and you will effect what abuse and denunciation have failed, and will forever fail, to accomplish; we mean, the emancipation of the negro in every country under the Dominion of the Saxon race.

BIBLIOGRAPHY AND RESEARCH SOURCES

Acuna, Rodolfo, *Occupied America: A History of Chicanos*, 1981

Adrian, Colton Jordan, *Capture of San Antonio*, nd

Albany Journal for 15 April 1836

Alexander, Barbara Zoe, *In Search of the Alamo Piper*, 1992

Allen, William W., Lawrence A B, *Texas in 1840, or the Emigrant's Guide to the New Republic: of Observations, Enquiry and Travel in that Beautiful Country*, 1840

Almonte, Juan Nepomuceno, *Almonte's Texas: Juan N Almonte's 1834 Inspection, Secret Report and Role in the 1836 Campaign*, 1836

Alsbury, Juana Navarro (Alamo Survivor): 1880s account

Alta California for 10 July 1876

Amador, General Juan Valentin Amador, letter dated 5 March 1836 at San Antonio

Ampudia, General Pedro de (Mexican Army): Eyewitness Account of 1836

Ancestry.com

Andrade, Juan José, *Informe sobre la Evacuacion de San Antonio de Bejar*, 1852

Archives@kent.gov.co.uk (Maidstone)

Baker, De Witt Clinton, *A Texas Scrap-Book. Made up of the History, Biography and Miscellany of Texas and Its People*, 1875

Baker, Karle Wilson, *Trailing the New Orleans Greys: South West Review*, April 1937

Barker Texas History Centre at the University of Texas in Austin

Barr, Alwyn, *Texans in Revolt: The Battle for San Antonio, 1835*, 1990

Barr, Alwyn, *Black Texans: A History of African Americans in Texas*, 1996

Barr, Amelia Edith, *Remember the Alamo*, 1888

Baugh, Virgil E., *Rendezvous at the Alamo: Highlights in the Lives of Bowie, Crockett and Travis*, 1960

Becerra, Francisco, *A Mexican Sergeant's Recollections of the Alamo and San Jacinto*, as told to John Salmon Ford, 1980

Belfast Newsletter for 19 May 1837

Bennet, Miles S., *Battle of Gonzales: The 'Lexington' of Revolution; published in the Quarterly of the Texas State Historical Association*, 1899

Bennett, Leonora, *Historical Sketch and Guide to the Alamo*, 1904

Blackwood's Edinburgh Magazine for January 1846 – *A Campaign in Texas*

Bowie, Walter Worthington, *The Bowie's and their Kindred: A Genealogical and Biographical History*, 1899

Brands, Henry William, *Lone Star Nation: The Epic Story of the Battle for Texas Independence*, 2004

Briscoe Center for American History, at the University of Texas in Austin

Brown, Gary, *Volunteers in the Texas Revolution: The New Orleans Greys*, 1999

Brown, John Henry, *History of Texas from 1685 to 1892*, 1892

Burrough, Brian; Tomlinson, Chris; Stanford, Jason, *Forget the Alamo: The Rise and Fall of An American Myth*, 2021

Buxton, Sir Thomas Fowell, *The African Slave Trade and Its Remedy*, 1840

Caledonian Mercury for 11 June 1836

Carey, Captain William Ridgeway (Alamo Defender), Letter written at San Antonio on 12 January 1836, and mailed at Natchitoches on 7 February 1836

Castañeda, Carlos Eduardo (translator and editor), *The Mexican Side of the Texas Revolution, by the Chief Mexican Participants (1836)*, 1928 – including *True Account of the First Texas Campaign* by General Santa Anna, Ramon Martinez Caro (Santa Anna's private secretary); General Vincente Filisola (Santa Anna's second in command); General Jose Urrea (Santa Anna's undefeated divisional commander); and General Jose Maria Tornel (Mexican secretary of war)

Census returns, 1841–1921

Centre for American History in Austin, Texas

Chariton, Wallace O., *100 Days in Texas – The Alamo Letters*, 1991

Chartrand, Rene, *Santa Anna's Mexican Army, 1821–48*, 2004

Cincinnati Enquirer for May 1876

Collins, Phil, *The Alamo and beyond: a Collector's Journey*, 2012

Colonial Magazine and Commercial Maritime Journal for 13 January 1841

Corner, William, *San Antonio de Bexar: A Guide and History*, 1890

Crockett, David, *Narrative of the Life of David Crockett, of the State of Tennessee*, 1834

Curtis, Gregory, *Forgery, Texas Style. Texas Monthly*, March 1989

Daily National Intelligencer for 11 June 1836, Reproduction of Sam Houston's Report on the Battle of San Jacinto

Daughters of the American Revolution, *The Alamo Heroes and Their Revolutionary Ancestors*, 1976

Daughters of the Republic of Texas Library, *Muster Rolls of the Texas Revolution*, 1986

Davis, Robert E., (editor), *Diary of William Barret Travis: Hero of the Alamo, August 30 1833–June 26 1834*, 1966

Davis, William C.,*Three Roads to the Alamo: The Lives and Fortunes of David Crockett, James Bowie and William Barret Travis*, 1998

De Bow's Review of the Southern and Western States: 'Early Life in the South-West – The Bowies', October 1852

Democratic Free Press (Detroit), Account by George M., Dolson after interview with General Juan Nepomuceno Almonte, 7 September 1836

DePalo, Jr, William A, *The Mexican National Army, 1822–1852*, 1997

Dickinson-Hanning, Susanna (Alamo Survivor): 1875

Donovan, James, *Blood of Heroes: The 13-Day Struggle for the Alamo – and the Sacrifice that Forged a Nation*, 2013

Duval, John Crittenden, *Early Times in Texas, or the Adventures of Jack Dobell*, 1986

Edmondson, J.R., *The Alamo Story: From Early History to Current Conflicts*, 2000

Edmondson, J.R., *Jim Bowie: Frontier Legend, Alamo Hero*, 2003

Ehrenburg, Herman Vollrath, *With Milam and Fannin: Adventures of a German Boy in Texas' Revolution*, 1843

Ehrenburg, Herman Vollrath, *Fahrten und Schicksale eines Deutschen in Texas (Journeys and Fates of a German in Texas)*, 1845

Ellis, Edward Sylvester, *The Life of Colonel David Crockett*, 1884

El Mosquito Mexicano (The Mexican Mosquito), 1834–1839

Esparza, Enrique, Article published in the *San Antonio Light*, 22 November 1902

Esparza, Francisco, Testimony given to Samuel S. Smith at Bexar County Court on 26 August 1859

Fehrenbach, T.R., *Lone Star: A History of Texas and the Texians*, 1968

Filisola, General Vincente, *Memoirs of the History of the War in Texas*, 1848–49

Findmypast.co.uk

Flack, Captain (The Texas Ranger), *The Texan Rifle Hunter or Field Sports on the Prairie*, 1866

Flack, Captain, *Texas Ranger: Or Real Life in the Backwoods*, 1866

Flannery, John Brendan, *The Irish Texans*, 1995

Flores, Richard R., *Remembering the Alamo: Memory, Modernity, and the Master Symbol*, 2002

Ford, John Salmon, *Origin and Fall of the Alamo*, 1896

Fort Worth Press for 14 March 1836

Genealogy.com

Gracy II, David B, *'Just As I Have Written It' – A Study of the Authenticity of the Manuscript of Jose Enrique de la Peña's Account of the Texas Campaign.'* Southwestern Historical Quarterly, July 2001

Gray, William Fairfax, *The Diary of William Fairfax Gray: From Virginia to Texas*, 1835

Green, Rena Maverick, *Samuel Maverick, Texan, 1803–1870. A Collection of Letters, Journals and Memoirs*, 1952

Groneman, Bill, *Defence of a Legend: Crockett and the de la Pena Diary*, 1994

Groneman, Bill, *Death of a Legend: The Myth and Mystery Surrounding the Death of Davy Crockett*, 1999

Groneman, Bill, *Eyewitness to the Alamo* (Revised Edition), 2001

Guerra, Mary Ann Noonan-, *San Fernando, Heart of San Antonio*, 1977

Guerra, Mary Ann Noonan-, *the Missions of San Antonio San Jose y San Miguel*, 1982

Guerra, Mary Ann Noonan-, *Heroes of the Alamo and Goliad. Revolutionaries on the Road to San Jacinto and Texas Independence*, 1987

Haliburton, Thomas Chandler, *Letter Bag of the Great Western, or Life on a Steamer*, 1840

Handbook of Tejano History

Handbook of Texas Online

Hansen, Todd, editor, *The Alamo Reader: A Study in History, including the Susanna Hennig (Dickinson) interview of September 23, 1876*, 2003

Hardin, Stephen L., and Zaboly, Gary S., *Texian Iliad: A Military History of the Texas Revolution, 1835–36*, 1994

Hardin, Stephen L., and McBride, Angus, *The Alamo 1836: Santa Anna's Texas Campaign*, 2001

Harrigan, Steven, *The Gates of the Alamo*, 2001

Harrigan, Steven, *Big Wonderful Thing: A History of Texas*, 2023

Harris, Dilui Rose, *Reminiscences of Dilui Rose Harris*, 1898

Haythornthwaite, Philip, and Hannon, Paul, *The Alamo and the Texan War of Independence, 1835–36 (Men at Arms)*

Hefter, Joseph, Angelina Nieto, and Mrs Nicholas Brown, *The Mexican Soldier, 1837–1847: Organisation, Dress and Equipment. Edited and Expanded by Patrick R Wilson*, 2013

Heitman, Francis B., *Historical Register and Dictionary of the United States Army* (2 volumes), 1903

Hobart Voice of Tasmania, 5 May 1951

Holley, Mary Austin, *History of Texas*, 1836

Hooker, T., *Uniforms of the Mexican Army, 1837–1847. Tradition Magazine*, 1976

Houston, Andrew Jackson, *Texas Independence*, 1938

Houston, General Sam, His official report on the battle of San Jacinto, 25 April 1836

Hoyt, Edwin P., *The Alamo: An Illustrated History*, 1999

Hudson, Hobart (editor), *A Composite of known Versions of the Journal of Doctor Joseph Henry Barnard, One of the Surgeons of Fannin's Regiment Covering the Period from December 1835 to June 5 1836*, 1949

Huffines, Alan C., *Blood of Noble Men: The Alamo Siege and Battle*, 1999

Hunnicutt, Helen, *A Mexican View of the Texas War. The Library Chronicle of the University of Texas*, 1951

Hunter, John Dunn, *Memoirs of Captivity among the Indians of North America from Childhood to the Age of Nineteen, with Anecdotes Descriptive of Their Manners and Customs*, 1824

Hunter, Robert Hancock, *Narrative of Robert Hancock Hunter, 1813–1902. From his Arrival in Texas, 1822, Through the Battle of San Jacinto, 1836*, 1966

Jackson Jnr, Ron J., and White, Lee Spencer, with a foreword by Collins, Phil, *Joe: the Slave Who Became an Alamo Legend*, 2015

Jenkins III, John Holmes (ed.), *The Papers of the Texas Revolution, 1835–1836*, 1973

Kennedy, William, *The Rise, Progress and Prospects of the Republic of Texas* (2 volumes), 1841

King, C. Richard, *Susanna Dickinson: Messenger of the Alamo*, 1976

Labadie, Nicholas Descomps, *San Jacinto Campaign, Texas Almanac*, 1859

Lamego, Miguel, and A. Sanchez, *Apuntes Para La Historic del Arma de Ingenieros en Mexico: Historia del Battalion de Zapadores*, 1949

Lamego, Miguel, and A. Sanchez, *The Siege and Taking of the Alamo*, 1968

Leach, James Henry, *The Life of Reuben Marmaduke Potter*, 1939

Lindley, Thomas Ricks, *Alamo Traces: New Evidence and New Conclusions*, 2003

Linenthal, Edward Tabor, *Sacred Ground: Americans and their Battlefields*, 1991

London Evening Chronicle for 10 February 1836

London Observer for 28 February 1915

Long, Charles, *The Alamo, 1836*, published by the Daughters of the Republic of Texas, 1981

Long, Jeff, *Duel of Eagles: The Mexican and US Fight for the Alamo*, 1990

Loranca, Sergeant Manuel, his account of 23 June 1878, taken from his journal

Lord, Walter, *A Time to Stand. The Epic of the Alamo*, 1961

Louisiana Advertiser for 28 March 1836

Lozano, Ruben Rendon, *Viva Tejas: The Story of the Tejanos, the Mexican-born Patriots of the Texas Revolution, with new material added by Mary Ann Noonan Guerra*, 1936 and 1985

McDonald, Archie P., *William Barret Travis: A Biography*, 1976

McDonald, David R., Juan Martin de Veramendi: Tejano Political and Business Leader, 2010

Magazine of American History for January 1878

Maillard, N Doran, *The History of the Republic of Texas, from the discovery of the country to the present time, and the cause of her separation from the Republic of Mexico*, 1842

Malet, David, *The Texas Revolution (1835–36)* in Oxford Academic, 2013

Matonvina, Timothy, *The Alamo Remembered: Tejano Accounts and Perspectives*, 1995

Michener, James A, *The Eagle and the Raven*, 1991

Miller, Edward L, *New Orleans and the Texas Revolution*, 2004

Morning Advertiser (London) for 7 June 1836

Morning Post (London) for 25 April 1836, 14 May 1836, 18 May 1836

Moquin, Wayne; Van Doren, Charles, *A Documentary History of the Mexican Americans*, 1971

Morphis, James M., *History of Texas, from its Discovery and Settlement, With a description of its principal Cities and Counties, and the Agricultural, Mineral, and Material Resources of the State*, 1875

Navarro, Carlos Sanchez-, *La Guerra de Tejas; Memorias de un Soldado*, 1938

Navarro, José Juan Sánchez- (Mexican Army), *The Texas War: Memories of a Soldier, 1831–1839*, 1938

Nelson, George, *The Alamo: An Illustrated History*, 1998

Newell, Reverend Chester, *History of the Revolution in Texas, Particularly the War of 1835 and '36*, 1838

New Orleans Advertiser for 28 March 1836

New Orleans True American for 29 March 1836

New York Tribune for September 1867

Nofi, Albert A., *The Alamo and the Texas War of Independence, September 30 1835 to April 21 1836*, 1992

North Melbourne Gazette for 11 August 1899

Nunez, Felix (Mexican Army), Article in the *San Antonio Light*, 1888

Olivera, Ruth R., and Lilane Crete, *Life in Mexico Under Santa Anna, 1822–1855*, 1991

Osterhout, Paul, *List of Those who fell in the Alamo, March 6, 1836*, undated

Pena, Lieutenant Colonel José Enrique de la: *With Santa Anna in Texas: A Personal Narrative of the Revolution*, 1975

PIX magazine for 30 June 1939

Potter, Reuben Marmaduke, *The Fall of the Alamo: A Reminiscence of the Revolution of Texas*, 1860

Ragsdale, Crystal Sasse, *Women and Children of the Alamo*, 1984

Reid, Stuart, *The Texan Army, 1835–36*, 2003

Ruiz, Francisco Antonio, *Fall of the Alamo, and Massacre of Travis and his Brave Associates* in the *Texas Almanac* for 1860; and the *San Antonio Light* for 6 March 1907

Salas, Elizabeth, *Soldaderas in the Mexican Military: Myth and History*, 1990

San Antonio Daily Express for 28 August 1904, 6 July 1906 and 12 May 1907

San Antonio Express-News, 13 September 1986

San Antonio Light for 19 February 1899, Account by Madame Candelaria

San Antonio Museum of Art

Santos, Richard G., *Santa Anna's Campaign Against Texas, 1835–36*, 1968

Schoelwer, Susan Prendergast, *Alamo Images Changing Perceptions of a Texas Experience*, 1917

Scoble, John, *Texas: It's Claims to be Recognised as an Independent Power by Great Britain, Examined in a Series of Letters*, 1840

Move this to H - Haliburton, Thomas Chandler, *Letter Bag of the Great Western, or Life on a Steamer*, 1840

Snyder, Betty Trammell, *Antebellum Arkansas, Trammell Families: Genealogical Sketches of Trammell Families in Arkansas, 1807–1850*, 1994

Sons of DeWitt County Texas

(The) South-Western Historical Quarterly, July 1932 to April 1933, July 1933 to April 1934, July 1942 to April 1943, July 1945 to April 1946, July 1990 to July 1991, July 1992 to April 1993, July 2000 to April 2001, July 2010 to April 2011

Sowell, Andrew Jackson: *Early Settlers and Indian Fighters of Southwest Texas*, 1900

St James Chronicle for 24 November 1835

Sutherland, Doctor John (Alamo Survivor): 1860

Sydney Gazette for 28 June 1836

Sydney Monitor for 24 February 1830

Teja, Jesus F. de la, *Faces of Bexar: Early San Antonio and Texas*, 2016

Telegraph and Texas Register for 24 March 1836

Texas Collection Library

Texas Monthly

Texas State Historical Association Quarterly

Thompson, Frank, *Alamo Movies*, 1990

Thompson, Frank, *The Alamo: A Cultural History*, 2001

Thompson, Frank, *The Alamo*, 2005

Thompson, Waddy, *Recollections of Mexico*, 1846

Todish, Timothy J.; Todish, Terry; Spring, Ted, *Alamo Sourcebook, 1836: A Comprehensive Guide to the Battle of the Alamo and the Texas Revolution*, 1998

Torget, Andrew J., *Seeds of Empire: Cotton, Slavery, and the Transformation of the Texas Borderlands, 1800–1850*, 2015

Travis, Colonel William Barret, Letters from the Alamo, 23, 24, 25 February 1836, and 3 March 1836

Tucker, Doctor Phillip Thomas, *Exodus from the Alamo: The Anatomy of the Last Stand Myth*, 2009

Tucker, Phillip Thomas, *The Alamo's Forgotten Defenders: The Remarkable Story of the Irish During the Texan Revolution*, 2016

Turbo, Silas Claiborne, *One of the Fearless Defenders of the Alamo*

Urizza, Colonel Fernando, His account recorded in 1859

Villanueva, Candelario, Testimony given to Samuel S Smith at Bexar County Court on 26 August 1859

Warwick Daily News in Queensland, on 7 October 1936

Williams, Amelia, *A Critical Study of the Siege of the Alamo and of the Personnel of its Defenders. South Western Historical Quarterly*, 1931

Wooten, Dudley G., *A Comprehensive History of Texas, 1685/1897 (two volumes)*, 1898

World's News for 26 November 1955

Yoakum, Henderson King, *History of Texas from its First Settlement in 1685 to its Annexation to the United States in 1846*, 1855

Yorba, Eulalia, Account published in the *San Antonio Express* for 12 April 1896

Zaboly, Gary S., *An Altar for their Sons: The Alamo and the Texas Revolution in Contemporary Newspaper Accounts*, 2011

Zavala, Adina de, *History and Legends of the Alamo and Other Missions in and around San Antonio*, 1917

INDEX